I Do

A Novel By

Angharad Jones

Bloomington, IN   Milton Keynes, UK

authorHOUSE®

AuthorHouse™
1663 Liberty Drive, Suite 200
Bloomington, IN 47403
www.authorhouse.com
Phone: 1-800-839-8640

AuthorHouse™ UK Ltd.
500 Avebury Boulevard
Central Milton Keynes, MK9 2BE
www.authorhouse.co.uk
Phone: 08001974150

First published by AuthorHouse 10/12/2006

ISBN: 1-4259-6266-1 (sc)

Printed in the United States of America
Bloomington, Indiana

This book is printed on acid-free paper.

1

September 2002

I woke now as I always did, fully dressed and alert, Sam was already up and in the kitchen that was never a good sign. Quickly I slipped my aching body from under the covers smoothing down my clothes as I went. Inhaling deeply I made my way into the kitchen, Sam stood beside the kettle.

"I need some money" his voice echoed around me

"Ok" I muttered, my body flinching at his tone.

"Don't look at me like that I need some money and I know you'll have some" his voice began to rumble through the walls.

"Ok how much?" I tried to keep my voice as light as possible.

"All of what you've got" he said bluntly, turning towards me.

The knot in my stomach tightened, I needed to stay calm

"I got paid today, so I'll give you the money when I come home from work" I said trying to smile, still he moved closer.

"I told you I need the money" he was in front of me now, his sweaty breath seeping into my skin.

"I can pop to the ATM now if you like" I said while trying to get out of his way.

As he lifted up his hand I stumbled, catching me with his other hand he held me to him, gently he stroked my dirty brown hair away from my eyes.

"Sweet innocent baby" his words didn't match the way he said them, tightening his grip he continued,

"If that's not too much trouble, go to the ATM and take out the money and then bring it to me." the emphasis of each word was unsettling, letting go of me he shoved me towards the door.

Sensing my escape I raced to my car, I knew that I would have to give him the money but I also know that he'd spend it all on booze leaving nothing for bills and food. Again I'd have to retain some money in secret. Pulling up to the ATM I pulled out my worn out card from a wallet that was never a gift to me. I knew that I could give Sam all my wage and still have $100 hidden. I had been paid a little extra it would at least help with paying for food.

When I got back to my home I was greeted by both Sam and Paul, but as soon as Paul saw me he hurried off. I felt sorry for him, it couldn't be easy for him, when he tried to help me he only got hurt. I knew that he couldn't leave completely because he'd be too worried about what would happen. At least I hoped that's why he never left, the idea that both of them enjoyed my pain was unthinkable.

"Here you are" I said handing him $365.00.

He snatched the notes from my hand, " that'll stop you eating crap and putting weight on" he looked at me in disgust before marching into our bedroom.

Defeated I slumped onto the breakfast bar stool, " why are you doing this to me?" I whispered.

"What?" he yelled into my ear, I hadn't heard him come up behind me but I didn't care I'd had enough, enough of him, enough of everything.

"Get up" he was yelling again.

I just shook my head, I was tired, tired of everything. I expected the punch but it never came, instead he moved away from me. Systemically he moved from room to room closing the windows as he went.

"I want a divorce" I heard myself shout.

Sam appeared from the bathroom, "we'll talk about this later" he hissed, before disappearing again. Running into our bedroom I grabbed the bag that lay hidden under our bed. I had threatened to leave him before in order to try and get him to see me, to actually see me. After the last time I never unpacked my bag it didn't hold any clothes I instead it only held paperwork and a few prized items.

"Give me your keys" he yelled

"No"

Gabbing hold of me Sam pushed me into the wardrobe I could see the hatred in his eyes and I guessed he could see mine.

Raising his arm, he asked if I wanted to be punched.

"No" I screamed the word so loud my throat felt as though it would be ripped apart.

His arm stopped and he drew back, questioning me with his stare that lasted only a few moments before he lurched at me. Dragging me by my shirt he pulled me from the bedroom to the veranda, as my feet slid along the polished wooden floor. Leaving me there he disappeared before reappearing after only a moment with my bag.

"I'll let you have this as long as you give me the keys" he spoke calmly now.

Looking down at my bag I handed him my keys.

Locking the front door behind him he dropped the bag at my feet.

"I'm going to take Paul to work I'll see you later" he hissed in my ear before joining Paul at the Ute.

On my own again I knew I had a choice to make and not much time to action it, I watched as they drove down the road. Where would I go? Who do I turn to? He'd be sure to find me anywhere in Australia and if he had to go looking for me that would make him really angry, more angry than he was now, maybe he would finally be angry enough to kill me although maybe then I'd actually get some peace. I had to think, looking down at my wallet it hit me, and I had to leave now otherwise I'd never escape. I had to go, I had to run and I knew just the person to help me be free. Running with all the strength that I could muster, I headed to the nearby hotels, through the path the lay between the neatly laid out houses and across the main road, there was no time to think any more. Now was the time for action, thinking could be done later, when I'm safe. Bursting in through the foyer of the nearest hotel I hurried over to the lady at the reception.

"I need a taxi, I've got to get away from my husband and fast, but I don't know any taxi numbers and my husbands locked me out of the house" the words fell from my mouth.

"Are you staying here?" she asked startled.

I knew from her question that I needed to make more sense.

"My husbands beats me, I need to leave him before he kills me, he's left the house locked up I don't know when he'll be back. I need a taxi now" stopping for breath I watched her eyes open wide, "please help me".

"You're not staying here?" she asked again.

I started to laugh, here I was making my bid for freedom and all she wanted to know was, was I staying at the hotel. Lifting up the shirt that I was wearing to the amazement of the people around me, I put my chest and stomach plus my multi-coloured bruises on view.

"My husband beats me, please can you order me a taxi" I tried again.

I guess she understood after all because as I smoothed down my shirt, she had the phone in her hand stretching it out to me.

I hurriedly instructed the taxi firm, before handing the phone back to her.

"Thank you" I yelled over my shoulder as I ran out the door.

I ran again back the way that I came, Sam hadn't returned yet. I grabbed my bag from the veranda and pulled it on to the street, where I waited. I knew that standing there would be my best chance, that way I could watch for who turned up first, my taxi or Sam. I waited for what seemed like hours, watching. Listening. I needed that taxi to get me to the bus station and then the bus to take me to the airport. I didn't allow myself to think about what would happen if something went wrong. This was a plan quite possibly one that would save my life. Looking up I watched as the yellow cab came towards me, allowing myself to relax for a second I quickly looked down the other end of the street. Reminding myself that Sam could turn up at any moment and when he did he would be mad.

"Are you going to the bus station?" the taxi man was talking to me.

"Yes, yes but please hurry" I begged him, shoving my bag into the cab before jumping into the passenger seat.

"Go" I shouted.

As we drove down the streets, I checked and double checked that we weren't being followed.

"If anybody asks you about me pretend that you never saw me" I advised him

"Why what you running away from?" he laughed.

Turning I looked straight at him, "my husband, he'll kill me if he gets hold of me and he certainly won't be giving you a pat on the back" my eyes confirmed the words I spoke.

"Ok" he muttered.

Passing through the streets of my home town, the rest of the journey was in silence, as we reached the bus station I handed over the money, grabbing my bag I looked into his face.

"Remember what I said"

"Yeah, didn't even see you mate" he said nodding his head, he had kind eyes.

"Good luck" he yelled after me as I slammed the door.

Looking around the bus terminal all I could see were normal looking people going about their normal happy lives, I had for far too long wanted to be one of them, scared, I joined the queue. Realising that all the normal successful looking women were reading magazines I grabbed one off the shelf.

"How can I help you?" the bored older lady asked from behind the counter.

"I need to get to Brisbane airport as quickly as possible" I said my voice shaking

"Well we have a bus that leaves on…"

Interrupting her I said "I want to get straight to the airport today I would like the next available bus"

"Ok, we have one that leaves in forty five minutes"

Aware of how abnormal I was acting I didn't really care. I waited for my change, then avoiding the stares of those around me I made my way to the waiting area. Searching for a good view point I sat down on a cold bench, placing myself in the position that I could see who was entering the terminal, no nasty surprises for me. I wanted to be fully aware of my surroundings.

Eventually the bus arrived and after quizzing the driver I felt comfortable enough to get on board, waiting for all the passengers to take their seats I chose two seats on their own. We needed to move quickly. What if Sam had returned? What if he knew where I was? Maybe he would think that I had gone on one of my walks along the beach. Maybe he wouldn't try and find me for a while, no he'd know exactly where to find me, and "God he could be in this building right now looking for me" I whispered to myself. Tying not to think anymore I opened the magazine that I had brought and tried to think hard about the supermodels with their beautiful lives, children, loving husbands. Out of all the stories that you hear about the famous people you never hear about one being beaten by the man that she loves. I guess that just made me feel weak, I was stupid, I was fat, I was ugly, I couldn't fuck, I couldn't even cook a steak the right way, what did anyone expect from me? Giving the magazine up as a bad idea I stared out of the window, I loved Caloundra and my heart began to ache, this was wrong I was having to say goodbye to a land that I had grown to want, to believe was my home land and now I was having to leave without even getting a chance to say goodbye. Lifting my hand up to my window I pretended to be touching all that I could see. It was my way of saying that I'd miss you but you will always be in my heart.

I was abruptly brought out of my thoughts by the driver, he'd stopped the bus, he'd actually pulled over like he was waiting for something. My heart began to race, what if Sam had stopped the bus, what if he had been flashing his lights at the bus driver to make him pull over. He could be out there right now, sweet talking the bus driver. Everyone would think that it was a scene out of a movie, but I'd know he'll kill me when he gets me home. I began to rock back and forth, my mouth had become so dry I couldn't open it; desperately I began to think of means of escape, where would I go? The airport, could I afford a taxi all the way there? The police? No that would really be a bad idea, I needed to think.

"Ok everyone off" came the drivers voice.

"What's happening?" I asked, my voice trembling

"You have to switch buses" came the reply.

"What?"

"Listen mate this bus that you're on doesn't take you to the airport and that's were you've paid to go, so you have to switch buses" the bus driver informed me.

"And the other one is going to the airport, you're sure about that?" I dumbly asked.

"Yes, yes, now get your stuff and get on the other bus" he ordered.

Reluctantly I made my way to the front of the bus. I still couldn't help the feeling that Sam had something to do with this. That maybe this was his plan to throw me off balance, to let me think that I'd made it and then he would be ready to pounce on me as soon as I got off the bus. With a deep breath I stepped from the bus, looking around me I hurried onto the second bus. I felt no hand on me, no commanding voice to tell me to stop in my tracks. He wasn't there, I was safe for the moment but now a new fear took hold of me, what if someone had seen me swapping buses? They would tell Sam, after all to see me out and about was strange. I had to be going to work or to and from the supermarket and it was quite clear that I was doing neither right now. Yet still no one questioned me, as far as I could tell, there were no spies on the bus who were ready to report my actions back to Sam, I seemed to be on the home run for now.

As the bus stopped outside the departures area at Brisbane airport I began to allow myself to smile, maybe I was going to make it after all. With no idea of what I was actually going to do or even what time it was, I walked into the departures area. With no ticket or means of buying one I couldn't go any further than the large hall where those lucky enough to hold a magic ticket waited for their turn.

"How did I think that I was going to get away? What the hell do I do now? Sam has to know by now that I'm not at home and it won't take him long to figure out where I am" I whispered to myself.

I need to think, I needed to weigh up my options, but I had to look normal. I had become aware that I was pacing, people were noticing me, and they could hear me muttering to myself. Heading towards the nearest café I ordered a super sized cup of coffee, something I thought might make me blend in with the other people around me. Although I guessed that people's heightened awareness had more to do with 9/11 I still didn't want to stand out any more than I already did.

Pulling out a torn piece of paper from my pocket I began to unfold it slowly, praising myself for keeping the number. Maybe I had known back then that this woman was going to save my life. Although I suspected the bond I felt with her had more to do with her accent reminding me of home more than anything I thought she could do for me. Yet there she was in black ink, Lisa, British Embassy, along with her work number and mobile. Expelling the air from my body I pretended to take a sip of my coffee. I felt guilty, she had tried to help me before but I had stayed with Sam. Maybe she wouldn't be able to help me this time, maybe she wouldn't want to, or worse still what if she no longer worked there? Looking down at the paper I knew that there was only one way to find out, I was going to have to ring her, all I had to lose was my life but I'd gotten used to those odds.

At the telephone bank I began to dial in the work number that she had given me the last time, I needn't have worried the phone was answered quickly.

"Hello I can I speak to Lisa?" I asked, interrupting the person on the other end of the phone.

"Lisa isn't here at the moment" came the reply, the voice soft with a slight Welsh note.

"Is there any way that I can get hold of her? It's really important, she promised me if I ever needed her all I had to do was call, do you know when she's back?" I was aware of how hysterical I had become, but I couldn't believe that after coming this far I would have no where else to turn.

"She's supposed to be here, have you tried her mobile?" the voice asked

"No I'll try that, thanks" the words barely left my mouth before I hung up, sometimes I could be so stupid.

Tracing the digits of her mobile number I typed then into the phone, "please god" I muttered

"Hello"

"Lisa?" I asked

"Yes, who's this?" she answered

"Mrs Williams, you helped me before" I answered

"What can I do for you?" she asked gingerly

I explained that this time I had left Sam for good, that he had put me into hospital, that he bruised me but most of all how scared I was that he would kill me. I told her about the guns and the knives and all the fights we had. I told her that he didn't, for the moment, know where I was and that I wanted to go home, that I wasn't safe to stay in Australia, after all I didn't have a death wish.

"What do you want me to do?" she asked, her voice silky soft.

"I want you to get me out of here, I've nothing, no money, nothing, I want to go home I don't want to die!" I pleaded

"Ok, I've got to get back to the office, can you phone me on the work number in ten minutes?"

"Yes, yes I can" I answered

Hanging up the phone I began to feel lighter almost as though I could do this, maybe I could make it home.

Ten minutes later I tried her work number, no answer, I tried again no answer, again and again I tried and still no answer, I began to panic. Shaking I typed in her mobile number, the phone was at first engaged, I tried again, no answer, the third time it appeared to have been switched off. I couldn't understand what was happening, she had asked me to phone her back in ten minutes hadn't she? Oh god what if she really didn't want to know, what if she was just saying she'd help just to get me off the phone. What the hell was I going to do without her help? I couldn't get home without a ticket and I had no money to purchase one. It seemed to me that the British Embassy were the only people who could send me home. My head started to spin, maybe if I went home now Sam wouldn't be there and I could pretend that I hadn't got as far as the airport this time. Maybe he wouldn't know, if I was lucky he would have been that angry with me, he would have decided to go out with his mates for a few hours and never have known that I'd gone. As appealing as that was to me, I knew that this was my chance, if I went back now I would be dead within months and yet I still needed to speak with him, explain what was happening. I didn't want him to go home to an empty house, I'm his wife, he had a right to know what I was doing, didn't he? I had to speak to him explain things then I would disappear, maybe go walkabout.

Without thinking much about the consequences I dialled my home number, if he were to pick up I would tell him that I was safe and that it was over before hanging up, simple really with no room for panic. The phone rung off, again I tried. He should know that its over between us, its only fair that I tell him, again the phone rung off. Panic gripped me, panic gripped me, my heart began to miss beats. What if he had already gone home and realised I wasn't there and had decided to come looking for me. He could be on his way now, he could be here now. Looking up from my seat I began to scan the giant hall, looking over to the queues I couldn't see him. Looking to the seats I couldn't see him, quickly looking behind me I couldn't see him. I dialled again and again and again, I dialled so many times that I felt sick there was still no answer. I needed him to answer, that way I could be sure that he was there and not here. Slamming the phone down, I stopped dialling, I needed to think, if he was on his way here I needed to move and fast.

Dialling Lisa's number again, she answered.

"Are you ok? It's been half an hour" she said worried.

"Yes I'm fine"

There and then we made our plan, she would phone my mother in England to arrange payment of the flight to get me home. I was to go down to the Qantas office and sign the documents to collect my ticket, someone would then escort me to the terminal and there I would board the plane. Simple really but it had to work, my mum had to be home to answer the phone, she had to be able to pay for the flight, they had to be able to get a flight and I had to be able to get on that flight and this had to be done before Sam turned up.

With my heart pumping I made my way to the Qantas office.

"I'm Mrs Williams, I'm meant to pick up a ticket from here to fly to England, the British Embassy in Brisbane should have phoned" I whispered.

A short, slim lady on the phone looked up,

"Yes, I'm talking to them now" she said

"Ok" I couldn't believe it, I was really doing this, maybe this could actually work.

The short lady stood up and offered the phone to me,

"Lisa wants to talk to you" she said

"Thanks" Shaking I took hold of the phone, "Lisa"

"Ok, I've spoken to your mum…"

"Oh god was she mad?" I asked

"No, no not at all although it is 5:30 in the morning over there" she laughed

"Shit she hates being woken up" I informed her

"A bit late for that now, she laughed, anyway your mum's paying for the airfare, so that's all sorted. All you have to do is get on the plane. Do you have your passport with you?" Lisa asked

"Yes, but it's expired, Sam would never allow me to get a new one" I told her as tears started to travel down my cheeks, I really needed a cig.

"That's fine, don't worry about that, now the lady at Qantas is going to look after you, you just make sure that you take care of yourself, good luck. Oh and another thing, your Mum's told me to tell you that she loves you very much"

With tears rolling down my cheeks I handed the phone back to the short lady, she introduced herself but I didn't hear.

"I need to go for a cigarette" I said to no one in particular

Jumping down from the seat I made my way to the nearest exit, my hands shook as I took out my crumpled pack of 25's and lit a cig, though now they were shaking out of a mixture of anticipation and fear. I was so happy to be going home, I needed to rest to get back to the person that I used to be. I was afraid not so much that Sam would turn up but that I might not make it back to England, I knew that I couldn't relax until my feet were firmly on English ground. I'd never been afraid to fly before, I had always loved the smell of airports, the excitement the wonderful feeling that would come over me. But now all I could think about was what if the plane crashed? Everything that I had done to get away from him would mean nothing if I didn't have the chance to tell people the truth. By now I had finished my third cig, I felt on the outside at least, a little calmer. Lighting my fourth and final cig, I inhaled deeply. Looking around me I knew that I would miss Australia very much, the country was my home. My life and I couldn't stay, "Aussie, Aussie, Aussie, oi, oi, oi" Smiling I threw the butt away and strode into the airport for the last time and without looking back.

I was marched up to the check in desk with security personnel, they had to be careful, after all I was going back to England from Australia with little luggage, I had no carry-on's the only ID that I has was an expired British passport and an Australian driving licence. I suppose that even though they knew why I was going back they had to be careful that I wasn't some kind of nutter. After check in I was lead to the departure gate, once there I was finally left on my own. Everything had happened so quickly from the moment I'd phoned Lisa it was taken out of my hands, I'm relieved that they did that, I'm not sure that after using so much of my strength to get that far that I could have done anymore. It didn't matter now, I was going back to England, acutely aware of people looking at me I smiled to myself. Who could blame them, I knew I looked a sight, I'd been in the same clothes all the day before, I'd slept in them, I had red swollen eyes, my long brown hair was matted and greasy and I had to be escorted to the departure gate by people with guns. Thinking about it, that's probably why no-one tried to talk to me, but I didn't care, I was lucky enough to be getting on a plane so quickly, I was lucky to have made it this far.

Walking towards the plane, I saw myself, what I had become. My body up front going through the motions while my inner self stayed behind a few steps. Wanting to stay, but also wanting to leave, not daring to look behind me I walked slowly, those around me growing increasingly inpatient with my progress. I could feel Sam's eyes boring into me or maybe I couldn't. I was sure that had Sam been there he would have called out to me. Yet maybe he wouldn't, maybe he was glad to see the back of me, he despised me, he had wanted me dead at times, so now I was doing him a favour. How I hated the idea of doing that man a favour. Maybe he hadn't seen me, he could be there right now searching for me. I decided not to turn and look for him, if he was there I didn't have the strength to explain yet again how unhappy he made me.

It was busy on board the plane, families going on holiday to the other side of the world, kids yelling hitting each other and generally annoying their harassed parents and other passengers. There were others who seemed sad that their holiday was over and that they would have to return to a wet, cold England, but still at least they had exciting stories to tell their friends and families. I, on the other hand had a hell of a lot explaining to do, but that didn't matter for now I had to do things in small steps the first of which was finding my seat.

With a little help I located my window seat, I wanted to be on my own but it looked that at least for the trip to Singapore I was going to have to sit next to a business man. Slumping into my seat I closed my eyes, but no sooner had I done that and my thoughts drifted to Sam. What if he didn't know that I was gone? He could be returning home right now to find that I wasn't there, he would be so very mad. Quickly I opened my eyes, I couldn't think about that right now I needed to think about myself, after all Sam hadn't thought too much about my feelings when he used his body to discipline me.

"Hi, Mrs Williams is there anything that I can get you?" the sweet voice drifted into my thoughts.

Turning to see who could possibly know my name I turned to see an air stewardess.

"I'm ok, I'm travelling to England on an expired passport, the ticket was bought not half an hour ago, Qantas helped arrange it, compassionate reason" I was doing it again I was such an idiot she didn't need to know all that why couldn't I answer a question with a simple answer, stupid.

"Yes, we know, that's fine. When we land in Singapore, if you could wait here someone will escort you to the next flight that will take you straight to England" she said, her face smiling.

"Ok" I muttered.

Turning away from her and the rest of the passengers I concentrated on what was out the window, I guess those sat near me all knew now that I was an 'interesting' passenger. I just hoped that none of them thought I was being thrown out of the country, or worse still think I was some sort of criminal. When finally the plane took off I allowed myself a few tears, how different this all was from my trip out to Australia. On my way out almost three years previously I had been so full of joy, how strange life can be.

"So why you travelling to England, business or pleasure?" asked the business man beside me.

Chit chat was something I'd forgotten how to do, it showed in my response,

"I'm going back to England, I've just left my husband, except I don't think he knows yet" I answered.

"Ok" he muttered before turning away and chatting to the man across the aisle.

I realised there and then I'd acquired a new skill of conversation killing.

2

1999

I meet a tall dark stranger, what more could a girl want? (a slap in the face from my future self!). I was out with my friends at my local pub and he was working behind the bar. He had beautiful smile, seemed shy around me somehow unsure of himself. Our first couple of weeks together were wonderful; he was my Wizard from Oz! He said all the right things, I actually felt special. I don't think I'd ever felt like that before, he made me feel loved, important, I knew that I was going to marry him! His name was Jesse, he was 28, he didn't have children or nieces or nephews and had never been married. He liked to have a good time with his friends getting drunk and playing the fool but he made me feel like a goddess, I'd melt every time he touched me. From the time we met we were inseparable, I had practically moved in with him much to my mothers disapproval! Life was always hectic he lived above the pub as well as working there so he never seemed to be without a drink and I drank to keep up with him.

A couple of weeks after we met, he'd finished locking up the pub at some hideous hour in the morning, late licence, and was having a couple of drinks to unwind. A few of the staff and a friend of mine were still finishing off their drinks, but Jesse was steadily worse. The landlord mentioned for him to go upstairs to the office for a chat, after what seemed like an age I followed to find Jesse in his room in a drunken state on the bed. I hadn't realised he'd drunk so much or maybe I'd drunk too much to know. Now this is where my memory goes a little hazy or maybe it really was the alcohol, regardless we argued over something, at the time I didn't know what he was on about. Suddenly he reached out and gripped my arm knocking me off balance before trying to hit me. The movement was sudden, I barely had time to respond when the land lord appeared in between us, yelling at me to get out. Our argument must have attracted quite some attention because as I left the room my friend was stood there asking me if I was alright but all I could hear was Jesse telling me that if I left now I wasn't welcome back. I didn't need telling again my friend's feet didn't even have chance to touch the ground as I hurried us out of there.

In the morning I explained to her what had happened and in my most convincing manner declared to her that it was all over between me and Jesse, there was no way I was going put myself through that kind of crap. I had more common sense than that, I wasn't about to let a man walk all over me. As I approached the pub I could feel my stomach doing somersaults I was nervous and yet I hadn't done anything wrong. As soon as I saw him those nerves disappeared and I began to feel bad for leaving him when he asked me not to, I felt sorry for him! I needn't have worried, from the moment that he saw me he hurried over saying how deeply sorry he was, how he'd understand if I didn't want to see him anymore. Somehow I felt cheated I wanted to be the one to say that what he had done was wrong and to tell him that I had no intention of seeing him anymore, but just as I thought to say what was growing inside me, he told me he had a secret that he needed to tell me because he thought that he could trust me. It was the reason for last night and why he behaved so strangely. I couldn't help it I had to know, so I followed him upstairs and into his room, I no longer felt scared of him I could see in his eyes how gentle and loving he was. And that's when he told me, at first I couldn't believe that he'd managed to get himself so worked up over it, so his name wasn't Jesse well not his first name anyway, he was Sam Jesse Williams, he wasn't 28 he was 30, neither of which was a big deal. We talked for hours and agreed that because we like each other so much we'd give it another go. So life went back to normal, I was with him when I wasn't working gradually losing touch with all my friends but I didn't care I was having the time of my life. We'd go out on day trips, go to clubs together, go on long drives to the middle of no where, I finally felt free.

One afternoon I was in his room alone when I noticed a picture that I hadn't seen before it struck me as odd. A tall, long blond haired man holding the hand of a little boy no more than a couple of years old, I couldn't help but pick the picture up for a closer inspection and then it hit me. The man in the photo was Sam but who was the child/he'd said he had no children, no nieces or nephews and why have a picture of yourself with a friend's child? Something that you have taken backpacking all over the world, it had to be special to him. As I stared at the photo I marvelled at how alike the child was to Sam, that's when I realised to my amusement that Sam had a son. As I was making up my mind on how to tackle him about the child, the decision was taken out of my hands, quite literally he had come in behind me and was now stood there picture in hand looking sheepish.

"Who's the boy?" I asked

"A nephew" he responded

"But you said you had no nieces or nephews" I stated puzzled

He just stood there

"Is he your son?"

He turned away

"I'm not angry just surprised, is he your son?"

"No"

Who is he then?"

"A friend's child"

I knew at this point that he was lying, he looked uncomfortable moving around the room,

"I know he's your son, he looks as handsome as you do"

"Really?"

"Why didn't you tell me?"

He then proceed to tell all about his son, and his ex partner who had disappeared with the child and hadn't been seen in a number of years despite attempts by Sam to track them down. He had been hearing through the grape vine that they were ok. She just didn't want to have anything more to do with him, he hadn't told me because he was worried that it make him sound like a bad dad, not seeing his son for years. Yet all I could think was how hard that must be for any parent to be without their child how that must make them feel jaded. I realised that this was a good a time as any to make sure that I had all the facts about him, before we carried on seeing each other.

"Is there anything else that you're keeping from me?" I asked as I sat him down.

"Well I'm not 30 I'm 34" he said with a smile on his face.

"Ok, is there anything else you think might upset me if you don't tell me right now?"

"No"

I asked to see his passport, his name was Sam Williams he was 36. I didn't walk away from him there and then instead I stayed because I loved him.

All the stories of him growing up with all the space to run around and be a child having fun, it made me wish so much that I could have know him then. The houses that he'd lived in made me believe how dull the ones I had grown up in, had been. Not that I had an unhappy childhood because I didn't but his just seemed so much more exciting. He talked about showing me the house that he had left behind, his Nan was living in it. It sounded wonderful set all on the ground level with hectares of land to the back of the house, where he had once kept horses. Not that I had ever had an interest in horses but some how it made it feel more romantic. The property was surrounded by a high fence all the way around, with the only access through the huge gates at the front of the property and up the long driveway. The picture that I developed in my mind was wondrous I couldn't wait to see the house that had a magnificent view of the lake opposite. Sam promised me that soon enough he would take me to see all the fabulous views that Australia had to offer.

I proposed to Sam, but not in the most romantic of ways, we were in bed, he was just lying there watching T.V. and as I looked at him I just thought how perfect it would be if we were married. Yet when I said it out loud I expected him to make fun of me, or move away from me as though I'd displeased him in some sense, but he didn't. He agreed and somehow we were engaged. I decided not to mention anything to my family just yet I needed to wait, to plan I was independent enough. I paid for the wedding rings and my engagement ring, it wasn't what I wanted not the perfect cut of diamonds entwined with gold. I didn't have that kind of money, but after all it wasn't what it's all about I had the perfect man in my life and family at the wedding. It may not have been every body's idea of a perfect wedding but it was my perfect wedding day. I was the princess for one day and my prince was charming in his kilt looking as much that dashing gentleman that dreams are made of.

With Sam's tales of how beautiful his home back in Australia was, his whole body sparkled when he discussed it with me, I couldn't wait for him to show me around where he grow up. We would visit his friends not his family, he was too worried that they would try and tell me lies about him. He did seem concerned about how I would feel leaving my family, but as I reminded him it was only going to be for three months then we planned on returning to England to run a pub together. I assured him no matter how dreadful some people might be we wouldn't have to put up with it for very long.

We purchased one way tickets, it was cheaper that way and also if we wanted we could come home a little earlier or even a little later. I did worry about the money, how we were going to support ourselves while we were out there, but as Sam told me again and again it wasn't really a concern after all he had a lot of businesses out there and some modest savings. If we did have to work that in itself would be an adventure. Our flight out to Australia was cramped and tiring, we booked very cheap tickets so we ended up with two stopovers. Besides have you ever tried to sleep on a plane, not an easy task unless of course you're lucky enough to be in first class, which I presume to be much easier with all that space, but I can't say for sure, as I've never been that lucky. Sam was so excited he behaved just like a child, although unlike a child he was knocking back drinks and chatting to other passengers regardless if they wanted to speak to him or not.

When we finally arrived and hurried to get our bags, all I was conscious of was my heart thumping in my chest. I was in Australia, the land of amazing beauty mixed in with seriously strange animals, with huge helpings of unbelievable magic in the shape of Ullaro and the Barrier Reef.

"What do we do now?" I asked Sam, unable to control the excitement in my voice.

"We go and see Nan" he smiled

"Where? How? Is someone going to meet us?"

"Err no I've just got to make some phone calls" he mumbled, walking away

I hurriedly followed him past all the other new arrivals and to the bank of payphones at the other side of the arrivals hall.

"So where are we again?........ I mean I know its Victoria but where in Victoria/" I still couldn't believe it.

Looking at me he tilted his head and grinned, "where at Tullmarine airport just outside Melbourne"

"Mmm Melbourne .. How far is it too yours?"

"Its not far to Nan's, maybe 30 km" he replied while feeding the payphone.

"Are we anywhere near a beach?"

"Look will you shut up, I've got to make some phone calls" he snapped before turning his back on me.

It didn't worry me that he seemed distant, I knew how much it meant to him that he was home and that his family got on well with me, I guessed he was a little uptight.

Five phone calls later he decided that we should get our money changed over and jump in a taxi.

"Is that all you've got?" Sam seemed surprised.

"Yes, we went through this before we left" I replied, feeling slightly annoyed.

"There isn't any hope in hell that money will last.....come lets go" Grabbing hold of my forearm he marched us out of the airport.

Although it seemed funny that he hadn't produced money to be exchanged, I just thought that he was waiting till later when ever that later would be.

Sept 2002

It appeared that closing my eyes wasn't going to be an option not unless I wanted to relive my life. My whole body was too tried to witness the pain, yet I knew that sooner or later I would give into the past.

"Would you like a drink?" it was the smiling stewardess

"Err yes a large white wine, if you have any" a drink, fantastic it would mean that I could concentrate my mind on the drink.

"Yes we do, dry?" she asked

"Yes"

Gratefully I took the glass from her, it was then that I realised why the flight had been so expensive, you certainly don't get free wine on a cheap flight, or maybe you do I was just being stupid again. Pulling down the table from the seat in front of me, I noticed for the first time that I had a T.V. inset in the head rest in front of me, looking around I noticed that everyone did, that was something else that you don't get on cheap flights. Usually you'd consider yourself lucky if you could actually get a decent view of the large screen towards the front of the plane without getting a painful neck. I couldn't help but be impressed and a little hopeful, I could keep myself occupied with this and maybe I can keep my mind from wondering over the mess that I had made of my life over the last three years. It was self evident now that the glass of wine was a bad idea, it was already gone and now all I wanted was a cigarette. We'd only been flying for at most a half an hour, I still had something like 16,000 miles to go before a nicotine hit was an option.

I located the headphones for the T.V. in the pocket of the seat in front, plugging it in was easy but finding something to watch was to become a nightmare. Lets see, I've just left my husband, I'm on a plane to England and really not in the mood for anything. As a standard rule airlines won't put on any movies that feature any sort of disaster apparently it upsets nervous folk, so what they tend to do is put on romantic love stories which wasn't something that I wanted to see. I don't want to be told by a movie that the only way for a woman to be truly happy is when a dashing man sweeps her off feet. I had that, a very dashing man swept me off my feet but then he showed his true colours, only when it was too late for me. I didn't need to be watching a movie full of women discussing their relationships and how they could have done better in order to stop the said dashing man from sweeping some other woman off her feet. I tried to do better, I tried everything I could, but instead of sweeping someone else off their feet or truly loving me for who I was, he just knocked me off my feet time and again. Switching the channels I located a sitcom channel, foolishly thinking that I was winning the battle. But no, this time the said dashing man had a beautiful, skinny, highly successful wife who could not only keep the house spotless, cook wonderful meals but was giving birth to a beautiful baby boy. I had failed on all those points. Turning over to the radio channels I again tried to find something that would distract, there was a choice of five love ballad channels, that wasn't going to work, a news channel, I didn't have the energy for anything heavy I had no compassion for other peoples plights. The comedy channel, now that was doable.

November 1999

As we arrived at the house, I was somewhat surprised it wasn't quite what I was expecting. I chose not to think of that too much, I was tired and needed sleep we had both been on the go for thirty-six hours and when you need sleep sometimes your mind can play tricks on you. We were greeted by Sam's Nan, she looked old and frail, I believed there and then we'd made the right choice to come and see her. Nan as I very quickly learnt to call her, seemed a little wary of me but what did I expect, after all she hadn't seen Sam for over two years and when she does see him again he's got himself married to some P.O.M. (Prisoner Of her Majesty). Very soon we were all chatting over a cup of tea in the lounge, Sam was showing her the wedding photos and I was pointing out who everyone was, yet I couldn't take my eyes off the inside of the house. It wasn't very grand, don't get me wrong it was lovely but it just wasn't what I was lead to believe. Or maybe I was just tired.

All too soon I woke to Sam shaking my arm

"You can't sleep here" he smiled, I'd fallen asleep on the settee.

Slowly I picked myself up and followed Sam to the room that would be ours, to my dismay it was full of junk. That wasn't what

I needed, I was shattered from the flight but now we had to get the room into some kind of usable order and make the bed, literally. Yet soon enough we were both sound asleep preparing our bodies for the adventure that lay ahead.

3

It didn't take long for more lies of my husband's to be uncovered, 'Im unsure now how it all came out but it soon became clear that there was more than one child in my husbands life. There was in fact two more children, two girls younger than his son, all three had different mothers. I didn't really believe him when he said all three mothers had disappeared and stopped him from seeing his children. I couldn't believe that all three women would do the same thing to him without some reason and I guess my suggestion that he should take some responsibility for not seeing his children should not have been voiced so loudly. The only real response that I got from him was screaming and shouting about how I couldn't possibly understand the stresses that he was under. How he had helped all three women and they had repaid him by taking his children away. How could I possibly understand after all I had no children of my own. I gave in to him, there wasn't any way that I was going to win the argument instead I just promised myself that I would somehow try to get him to understand that he could if he chose to, make contact with his children and I would support him in however he chose to go about it.

We decided to stay in Australia a little longer than originally planned, but we needed some money to do it and so I found myself looking for a job. This was my most stressful time by far, we had only been in Australia for three months but our arguments started from the moment it was decided I would get a job. Sam took me down to the local Centrelink office so that I could type out my C.V., while he saw some friends. I felt nervous, I was in a strange country and I didn't really know what to expect from the job process, although I worked in England I didn't know if it would be the same in Australia. When Sam returned home I showed him the C.V. that I'd spent almost three hours making perfect, only for him to point out what was wrong with it. I had to stop thinking about how was in done in England I had to sell myself better, after all I could say things that weren't necessarily true because he felt it was unlikely they'd bother to check. I hated that idea , I had good work experience, I was good at any job that I put myself to. I hated the idea of not telling the truth, it just didn't seem right. So we came to a compromise, if I couldn't find a job in one week with my C.V. the way it was I had to rework it to Sam's specifications.

I got a job within the week working at a supermarket, which is what I expected, it didn't matter what country a supermarket is in they all work the same. My happiness didn't last long before me and Sam started arguing over the job. I couldn't understand the big deal it was a job. Ok it wasn't full time, didn't pay fantastic money and I needed Sam to drive me back and forth, but the way I saw it, it was a start, it brought money in and gave me a work history in Australia. I knew that there wasn't any reason why I couldn't look for the perfect job in the meantime. As I told Sam if the money was such a problem why didn't he start looking for work him self, so deciding he would show me how it was done he started to look for work.

Sept 2002

My mind was doing it again, I didn't need to rerun the past three years, I knew where I went wrong. I was useless at so many things, I was an embarrassment to my husband, people pitied him, to have a wife that was unable to cook, who had no skills that made her employable, who couldn't even keep the home clean. It was clear to me that if I was going to survive this flight I needed something to concentrate on. I began to flick through the channels again, hoping to find a cop show that I could watch for half an hour or so and rest my mind. Looking to my left I noticed that the business man had what looked like a computer game on his screen, realising that I must have missed at least one channel I was full of renewed hope.

Suddenly there it was, except it wasn't a computer game. It was actually a channel showing where our plane was, how long we'd been in the air for, how far we'd travelled, our estimated time of arrival and so much more. This would be my saviour, I could now track my progress I could watch it for the whole flight, I could will the plane to move faster. To my dismay when I checked on the map how far I had travelled it couldn't have been any longer than my thumb width. Yet there I was being stupid again, slowly I traced the route that we had taken so far, it took me right back to the east coast of Australia, to where my home had been. My stomach began to do somersaults, I was aching all over, here I was running away from a land that I had grown to love. Australia was my home, I was almost a permanent resident I had already counted myself as an Australian. Unless of course England was playing Australia at rugby and then the lines became a little blurred. I hadn't wanted to leave and now I had no idea if I was ever going to see my home again. Would I ever be able to drive the Great Ocean Road again or travel across the country from Melbourne to Brisbane, to be greeted on my paddocks by Kangaroos? Or would I ever master the technique of doing a right hand turn by using left hand lane in Melbourne?

April 2000

Our first home together was meant to be a new start for the both of us, as a couple and individuals, I had grown to love the idea of starting a new life with Sam in Australia. I missed my family but it was exciting, thrilling even. Our fights had been about his frustration at being stuck in one room not being able to support me, but now it would be different he had got himself a truck in order that he could make a living from being a courier. He could now be the husband that he longed to be, supporting his wife, he was old fashioned like that. We moved only a few miles away from his Nan into the nearby town, close enough for me to walk to the train station, closer to Sam's friends.

The day that we moved in two of his friends came round, looking back I wished that I'd never laid eyes on Paul, from the moment that Sam introduced us there were problems. I'd always managed to side step the paranoia of my husband, but with Paul it was different, when ever Paul came round to see Sam I made excuses not to be in the same room as him. I wasn't attracted to him, I loved my husband, but that never seemed to matter to him. It simply didn't matter who it was, male or female Sam just thought that by the way that I looked at them I must want to sleep with them. It was simply easier just not to look at anyone, I had the man that I loved and he loved me.

Paul was a cousin of sorts, they had grown up together, their mothers had been firm friends. Sam believed everything that Paul told him, which I found intolerable. We began to argue over Paul, Sam was making it impossible for me to say anything about his cousin. I was either being too nice therefore I must want to sleep with him or I'm being nasty and I had no right to be nasty about him. Even as stupid as I was it didn't take me long to realise that the safest way was to say nothing at all, besides I had other things to worry myself with.

I wasn't the tidiest of people and with the hours that I was working I didn't always have the energy to worry about clothes on the floor or plates on the side. I didn't know about having to move everything off the worktops every time you cleaned, I hadn't seen the point in spending hours upon hours ironing everything perfectly, making sure that you put the creases on a shirt in exactly the right places and then making sure that there wasn't any creases in jeans and some t-shirts.

Sept. 2002

"Would you like some food?" the stewardess was back

"no thank you" I replied, putting my hand up to stop the plate from coming anywhere near me. I couldn't stand the idea of any food what so ever, but aeroplane food was certainly out of the question.

When the business man started to open his package, the smells began to swirl around me, I'd made the right choice. It wasn't that I wasn't hungry, but for so long I only ate when it was safe to do so and for now it wasn't safe.

2000

I can still remember the first time that he was physical with me, other time have been fused together, yet the very first time is crystal clear in my memory. As usual on a Saturday morning Sam stayed in bed recovering from the night before, while hissing at me to get his breakfast perfect. I hate poached eggs. I took him in a mug of tea, not daring to look him in the eye, I wasn't in the mood for a confrontation, he barely acknowledged me. I then took in the knives and forks along with the salt and pepper, god how I hated his need to eat in bed, he stank. I walking into the room for the last time with his and my full English breakfasts. He didn't look at me, just started to eat, shovelling the food into his gob. I finished and had decided to get on with the housework it needed to be done, after all if I didn't do it, I was useless.

I had started to wash up when he called for me,

"Get me another tea babe"

"Coming" I resented him doing this, because I knew he'd spend the rest of the day telling me to do things for him, then yell at me because I hadn't done everything he said I should, like a good little wife.

As I took him in another cup of tea I could sense that there was going to be problems, I wasn't in the mood.

"Have you seen the state of the bathroom?" he yelled in my ear, as I lent forward to put his mug down.

"I know, I'll get round to it"

"Haven't you finished the kitchen yet? He grabbed my arm, Are you stupid?"

"No" That was the wrong thing to say, sometimes I could be so stupid, if I hadn't said anything it would have been fine, but no I had to go ahead and open my stupid mouth.

Sam had let go of my arm and shoved me to the side like I was nothing but a piece of dirt to him, thankfully he didn't say anything. I stupidly thought that I'd got away with it, that he hadn't noticed. I moved slowly out of the bedroom and along the corridor and into the kitchen.

Sam's voice boomed down the corridor and bounced around my head.

"You're fucking useless, all I'm trying to do is teach you how to do things properly and you're just an ungrateful P.O.M."

My heart started beating faster, I wanted to say something, anything to defend myself but I'd already said too much. Quickly I grabbed the cleaning clothes and sprays and hurried back down the corridor and into the bathroom, which lay directly opposite our bedroom.

"It's too fucking late now, you're just a fucking lazy P.O.M., I've had to teach you everything"

I hated it when his voice went calm, it showed how really pissed off he was, I just had to make sure that I did what he wanted all day. I quickly started on the bathroom, I knew it was going to have to be gleaming, 'why had I said anything?'

It was then that I felt the cold dampness of fear as it trickled down my neck, this was strange, wrong. With a whoosh of air my head was flying forward into the sink, I could feel the hairs on my head coming out as he twisted the strands into his knotted fingers. My head never did hit the sink, he stopped it within centimetres.

"You think that you're so special don't you?" his voice had become quiet, menacingly so.

My head was beginning to hurt.

"Stop please, you're hurting me" I pleaded, lifting my arms up to his.

"I know what you're like, I know you better than you know you're self and you'r an ungrateful P.O.M."

29

I was beginning to move back, 'what was he doing?' Next thing that I knew I was lying on the floor with Sam stood over me, still holding my hair. Looking into his eyes I could see the hate that his spiteful words were confirming to me.

"This bathroom look fucking awful...not even using the right cleaning products.... How can I trust you to keep a good home..... you're my wife for fucks sake....I don't even know why I married you...you were nothing when I met you... I knew teaching you was going to be hard work.... But you're an ungrateful P.O.M."

He was dragging me by my hair, from the bathroom into the corridor, I closed my eyes so that I wouldn't have to see the hate although I could still hear it.

"I know that you're sleeping around you fucking slut"

My mind was racing I hadn't done anything of the sort, I hadn't even thought about doing it,

"I haven't" I yelled back at him.

He stopped, let go and stood over my shaking body, bending over he looked straight into my eyes;

"Fucking shut it, you stupid, fat, ugly cow" he spat the words into my face. Grabbing hold of my arm with one hand and grabbing my neck with the other he pulled me up off the floor and marched me backwards into our bedroom, where he pushed me down onto the bed.

As I lay there I allowed myself to think that he'd finished, that he had got whatever it was out of his system and that he'd allow me to go back to the housework. He worked fast as he took my trousers off and throw them out the bedroom door.

"What are you doing?" I mumbled

Stopping he looked at me,

"I'm going to sniff you"

The words rattled around my head, 'sniff me' what did he mean? I tried to push off, fight back but he just used one arm to pin me down, you see he was 6" 4 and 16 stone and I was 5" 6 and 9 stone. Soon he had my knickers off, I lay there not daring to look at him. This wasn't the man that I had fallen in love with. I tried to think of when we had first met how beautiful he had been, when I could feel the sensation of air between my legs. I moved my head to see what he was doing.

30

I could move my head but the rest of my body didn't follow because still his arm pushed down on my chest. Then the air moved a couple of inches up, with each I wanted to be sick.

"Get off me" I screamed, almost instantly wishing that I hadn't. For as soon as the words left my dry mouth I could feel a sharp pain. He had bitten me. I turned my head to the wall and allowed the tears of pain, confusion and fear to travel down my cheeks and puddle on the bedcovers.

Slowly the sensation of his breath crept up my body, the sense that he was climbing on top of me was confirmed when I felt him between my legs.

"I had to sniff you, his voice was gentle now, I had to know if you'd been with anyone else"

I didn't look at him, I couldn't, I needed to be sick.

"You see I love you, I just couldn't bear the thought of you with some one else...look at me" his fingers dug into my cheeks as he turned my face to his.

He was smiling now his eyes were full of kindness, gradually he forced himself into me moving slowly in and out.

"I love you" he whispered into my ear, my body was numb now. I just wished it would be over soon. Gradually his breath became faster as his breathing matched his movements. Holding me down he lifted his body up as he pounded my aching shell, finally throwing himself forward his cum gushed out of me.

Laying there with his full weight on top of me I could feel his sweat from his chest dripping down my cheek suffocating me.

"Come here and let me cuddle you" he whispered as he moved off me. Lifting myself up I looked down at my legs I wasn't sure what I expected to see but I did expect to see something, some indication of what he'd just done to me. Yet there was no bruises just red marks and no blood just his fluids trickling between my legs. Head down I manoeuvred myself over to him, I didn't dare look at his face, I dare not let him know what I was thinking, what if I was wrong? After all I wasn't very good at many things and he was my husband, and a husband who indeed put up with my mistakes. He couldn't help it if he lost his temper some times everybody does, I was the worst for doing it I could be an absolute bitch. Laying there I allowed myself to drift away to happier days, when Sam wasn't so angry with the world.

The morning after, I was awake long before Sam, but I just laid there waiting for him to wake I didn't want to upset him again, he'd already told me I wasn't going to work for a few days, he thought it important that I stayed at home with him. As I moved to lay on my side facing the wall, my privates hurt, I guessed the pain was from him biting me, but I couldn't see if there was any damage done, it was just the pain that remained with me.

Ordering me out of bed, Sam's voice cut into my dreams like a knife, I guessed it was time to get up. Moving around the house I dressed in a dream like state, looking at myself in the mirror frightened me.

"Where are you going?" I asked, my voice unsteady.

"I've got to work and after your display yesterday you're coming with me" he stated, pulling on his shirt.

'My display', the words swam round my head while I showered and got dressed.

"You look like shit" he said throwing a hat at me, "wear this, it'll cover you're face"

Looking at him quizzically, I wasn't sure what he meant after all he hadn't hit me in the face. I darted into the bathroom and looked at my face in the mirror. I couldn't help but smile, my face was puffy and swollen, "never go to bed crying" I thought to myself, "it will always leave you looking like shit the next day" with me it always left the tail-tail sign on my face.

"Come on" Sam yelled from the door, running I met him at the truck. "Put it on" he nodded to the hat that I held tightly in my hand. A little wave of satisfaction swept over me, he was ashamed at the way that I looked knowing that he was the one reasonable for it. Quickly I pulled the hat on over my ears and zipped my jacket up over my mouth until only my nose and eyes could be seen.

4

Sept 2002

Pulling myself up in the chair I realised that being in this cramped position there was no escape for my thoughts, I would have to embrace them whenever they arose. Yet for now I fancied my chances again with the TV, in front of me. 'Spider-man', I smiled to myself, some boys never really grow up, but what was really scary is that some of these boys end up in positions of great influence. It had to be a man who decided, 'hey you know what, why don't we make a spider-man movie', didn't it? Feeling like I'd finally found something to watch that required no mental strain I began to relax a little. It didn't take me long to pick faults with the characters. There was spider-man, with all his powers to do good and to help others but he's still not happy. I know that it's not real but it stilled gnawed away at me. Why was it that those who have the world at their feet, make believe or not, still had the 'why me' attitude. I suppose the grass is always greener elsewhere.

2000

Life became the same process each day, I would wake, go to the train station and go to work making sure that I didn't talk with anyone. I would come home and clean up any mess that had been left by Sam, I would then cook his tea before cleaning down the kitchen. Hoover, clean the bathroom, talk only when spoken to, smile and laugh in the right places, take the blame for the neighbours, for my dog and for anyone or anything that I should have realised would cause Sam embarrassment. I hated the weekends, we had two choices for weekends both were equally bad in my eyes, the first simply if we were home for the weekend I had lots of work to do. I would get up early on Saturday mornings to cook Sam his breakfast, I hate poached eggs, then feed it to him in bed. The rest of the day was taken up with cleaning every room in the house from floor to ceiling. Moving every item so that the worktops and window sills could be disinfected, cupboard doors cleaned down, the floors vacuumed (on my hands and knees). Washing clothes, drying clothes, ironing clothes, cooking the perfect steak, food shopping.

It wasn't always bad between us, sometimes we had weeks of happiness. Our weekends away were special, as Sam had promised me, we saw what Australia has to offer. My favourite trips were our weekends away in Sorrento and Rye. You could see so much in the car on the way there. It was usually dark when we arrived, but we'd pitch our tent along our favourite stretch of beach. If I was lucky Sam wouldn't go straight to the nearest pub, he'd spend the evening with me. I felt close to him on those nights as we'd walk along the starlit beech. The smell of the ocean was intoxicating, I wished those nights would never end. If luck was on my side we would make our way back to the tent laughing and kissing, have a beer then slide into bed. Those times were precious to me, they made me believe that Sam truly loved me and that all our silly arguments meant nothing when it was just him and me together.

If though I was unlucky, Sam would want a beer and lots of it, I hated that. I longed for the times that it was just me and him, for our intimate moments when we would talk and hold each other. But as Sam said I was just being selfish, after all our weekends away were for the both of us to enjoy and do what makes us happy so he was right with that reason in mind I was selfish to want him all to myself. I soon got used to the idea that when I'd wake up in the morning, Sam was already planning his day and that by the time I'd return from the shower block he would be gone. At times I was grateful, knowing that I wouldn't see him for the rest of the day and that when he did return he would be in a good mood because he'd done what he wanted. Yet I resented him for it to, while he was out and about doing what he wanted I had to stay near the tent, it was safer for me there. It could have been so boring but I did have the most beautiful beach on my doorstep. The rays of the sun would dance along the water, enchanting those who looked. Yet I had no one to share those moments with, I longed to talk to someone but that was never a good idea. If I so much as said 'good morning', Sam always appeared in order to warn me off. I had become a master of talking with myself, which only confirmed what Sam said, I was insane.

Sept 2002

Watching the smiling, beautiful people glide around on the screen in front of me, made me feel so jealous. I wished that just for one day my life could be that simple and that nothing could harm me. Instead I'd been spending my days feeling scared, angry and confused. I wished I could be like the female character in front of my eyes. There she was thinking that her life was over all because she'd been stood up! Why couldn't my life be that easy, some people really don't know how it feels to be so low that you don't want to live anymore.

2000

"You fucking stupid bitch" Sam pushed me away. Sitting back into his chair he shook his head before switching over the TV channel. "Why does he never see me? I don't understand". I had began to cry silent tears, I hated that I was weak, I hated that I wanted him to hold me, to feel the real me not just the person he wants me to be. My breathing had began to slow, in an almost eerie fashion my body began to calm down, yet my mind raced. Looking up I found myself in the bathroom, the only room in the house that when I cried nobody would yell at me, tease me or hurt me. It was safe, the door behind, sink in front, mirror above, bath to my right. I watched in the mirror as a tear made its elegant path down my face. God I hated myself, I was stupid, I was ugly, fat, with the frustration running through my veins I slapped the wall only to let out a groan at my weakness at not even being able to punch it. I hated myself. Ashamed I looked down at the sink, I hadn't realised that I had gripped hold of it, let alone how tightly I was holding on.

"What you fucking doing now?" Sam's voice echoed around my haven.

"Cleaning" I called back, why did he always have to yell? I may have been many things but I wasn't deaf.

"Good"

My head was screaming, why did he do this to me? Why did he hurt me?. I needed to do something to make him actually see me, to see me hurting. It needed to be something that would hurt him too. Just then I noticed the silver of the nail scissors and smiled, 'perfect' I whispered.

Carefully I lifted the scissors, I was surprised at how calm I was. Taking hold of my long brown hair in one hand and the scissors in the other, taking a deep breath I began to cut, cursing I made a mental note that the kitchen scissors would have made a far better job. Once I was satisfied I placed the scissors back where I found them and scoped up the hair that now lay in the sink and on the floor. All the while hoping that it would work, after all Sam hated seeing me hurt or damaged unless of cause he was "teaching me". Gingerly I made my way back to the lounge, where Sam sat laughing at the TV.

"Sam" I said

"What?" he didn't even take his eyes off the TV.

"I've cut my hair" my voice was a whisper now, I'd lost my bottle.

"What?" he asked.

Taking a step back I tried again

"I've cut my hair" I answered

"I heard you the first time....why?" he asked and yet he still hadn't moved from his seat.

"I was angry"

"Why?" he asked, his face showing only a flash of concern.

"The arguments"

"So you cut your hair!"

"Yes"

Sam still hadn't moved from his seat, he studied my shaking figure, after what seemed like a life time he spoke up.

"Go and get the kitchens scissors and turn on the light"

"Why? What are you going to do?" I asked gingerly.

"Just do it" he barked

Turning sharply on my heels I rushed into the kitchen, grabbing the scissors I hurried back, flickering on the light as I went past.

"Come and sit here in front of me I want to see how bad it is" he patted the place in front of him.

Sitting down, I handed him the scissors, I reasoned that my plan had worked. That he would see the real me. Gently he combed my hair with his fingertips, I could hear the scissors click as he cut.

"I'm just sorting out the ends for you" he informed me.

Gathering my courage I decided to speak.

"I'm sorry, it's just that I've felt so alone, it's almost as though you don't even know I exist anymore, it's stupid I know but I needed to do something to get you to see me"

"All done, now piss off" he whispered into my ear.

It had almost worked, or maybe the truth was I was just mad, Sam would see it that way. Gathering my things I retreated into the bedroom, sometimes I was truly stupid.

Sept 2002

Growing up, I had always been happy with being me. I didn't find myself wanting to be like my friends, I loved that I was different. I was happy when people would say that me and my friends were so different from each other. To me it made our friendships work better, being good at different things meant that we helped each other, cared for one another, but now things were different, I had changed. As I looked around the other passengers on the plane, I longed to be like them. Like the family in front of me, they were on their way home from a months long holiday. So full of hope and happiness that I envied them and yet my brain was telling me that things are not always what they seem. How was I to know what was happening inside these peoples heads. Maybe there was someone on the plane who understood the hurt that I was feeling. After all if there was one thing that I had learnt for myself was that life is not black and white, decisions are made each day that have a ripple effect on everyone.

2000

I didn't know where he was, although I had a fair idea it would probably be the pub. It was an educated guess. I phoned him. No answer. I continued to worry for him, he said he was only popping out to see a mate but I should have know better. I still wanted to believe him and sometimes 'popping' out would mean he was back in minutes. As the weeks went on though it wasn't unusual for him to be gone for hours, always returning drunk. It worried me that he would drive, I loved him with all my heart but I worried constantly that he'd crash the car and kill himself, or that he'd kill someone else, or that the police would pick him up for drink driving. I worried about his and other peoples safety but I'm ashamed to say that I worried about my safety more. If he returned home drunk then I would know about it.

I didn't blame those that drank with him, I got on well with them and it wasn't their place to take care of him. I tried phoning him again and still he didn't answer, which only made me worry about him more. I had tried so many times to explain to Sam that I wasn't nagging him I was just worried about his safety and that I loved him. As the night went on, I grew tired, it seemed obvious to me this was going to be a long night. I needed to get some sleep, because if Sam was up to his usual then when he got home I would have to keep him company. Regardless of what kind of state he was in I knew that I couldn't go to bed naked, just in case he thought I'd screwed someone while he was out. The best reason though for not going to bed naked was Sam's drunkenness, I hated being dragged out of bed naked, it was humiliating.

I'd barely been in bed ten minutes, when the headlights from the Ute moved across the ceiling. Reaching my arm across the floor I located my trousers that I'd placed there earlier. Quickly I manoeuvred them under the duna and slipped them on. Still I hadn't heard the front door, looking towards the curtains I noticed more lights from outside. The knocking on the front door diverted my attention, quickly I walked to the source of the noise.

"It's me. I haven't got my key" Sam slurred through the wood.

Turning on my heels I headed quickly to the bedroom, where I'd left my set.

"I'm coming" I called out to him.

"Come on" He called, while continuing to bash on the door.

No sooner had I clicked the lock, than the door swung inwards knocking me off balance. While my eyes adjusted to what I saw, I was disappointed. In front of me stood Sam looking like he'd tried to drown himself in beer, either side of him stood two police officers.

"Hi babe" Sam slurred.

Ignoring him I moved forward, glancing quickly to my left I could see the Ute was there and seemingly one piece.

"Move back" ordered the female officer

Looking at her I couldn't help but raise my eyebrows, it amused me that she felt a need to bark orders at me but I guessed she was the 'bad' cop.

"Are you Mrs Williams?" asked the male officer

"Yes" I answered.

"Is this man your husband?" he asked

"Yes" I answered again

"We've reason to believe he has been driving while under the influence" the man continued.

"Look do you mind if I put some clothes on" I said while closing the door, I was still naked from the waist up.

"Of cause, we have to take Mr Williams to the station" he replied.

"Ok" I smiled and closed the door. I really wasn't bothered the longer they had him the better it was for me, besides I was more irritated by the officers behaviour she was rude and all he wanted was a perve, but that's the good cop, bad cop game.

Making myself a cup of tea I pulled a t-shirt on over my head, reasoning with myself I allowed myself to believe that this might actually be the wake up call Sam needs. After all I couldn't drive and if he wasn't allowed to, it certainly would limit where he went and what he did. One thing for certain though I wouldn't be mentioning to Sam that the cop had been able to have a real good perve. Suddenly the noise of the doorbell dragged me away from my thoughts.

"It couldn't be Sam back already could it?" I whispered to myself.

I opened the door to the same male police officer that had been perving.

"Where's my husband?" I asked looking behind him.

"He's at the police station, I've come to ask you a few questions" he sated, while striding into my house.

"Are you on your own?" I asked his back as I watched him move into my house.

"Yes" he replied.

"Oh good, that woman that you were with seemed to have issues" I said sarcastically as I closed the door.

Quickly he spun round,

"What do you mean?"

"Nothing" I smiled at him before dismissing the comment with my hand.

I pointed him into the kitchen and towards the breakfast bar,

"Would you like a tea or coffee?" I asked.

"No I'm just here to ask you some questions" he responded while making himself comfortable at the breakfast bar.

"Well I don't know what I can tell you, the first that I knew was when you were at my door, I've been asleep " I stated. I felt sorry for the officer, it seemed obvious that they needed more information in order to charge Sam. Yet no matter how glad I was that he was out of my hair for a little while there was no way that I was going to give them anything. I didn't have a death wish.

"What time did your husband leave the house today?" he asked

"I don't know" I replied

"Where was he going?"

"I don't know"

"Do you know who he was with?"

"If he was with anyone, it could be any number of people" I replied there was no way that I was getting anyone else into trouble.

"Did your husband arrange for a lift tonight?"

"I don't know, I was asleep" I answered while lighting another cigarette.

"Did you see anyone drop your husband off home tonight?" the officer seemed to be getting annoyed.

"No I was asleep"

"Is there anything you can tell us about your husbands whereabouts tonight?" he asked, looking straight at me.

"Well he went out, I'm not really sure when. Then the next thing that I can be sure of was seeing you, your partner and my husband on my doorstep"

"Can you not tell us anything else?" he asked rather shocked.

"No, nothing that comes to mind, sorry" I apologised to him.

"Well thank you for your time" he said as he pushed the stool away.

"When do you think you'll be done with him?" I asked as I showed him out.

"Shouldn't be long" he answered.

"Good" I said as I closed the door in his face. It wasn't that I dislike the police, I just knew my place and that I couldn't afford to offend those who knew my husband, I rather like my head being attached to my body.

5

2000

After one practically bad day or maybe just another same old day, Sam did what he did best and disappeared down the pub and again I was left feeling angry and confused. I hated it that Sam would get so angry with my stupidity that he couldn't even bear being in the same house as me, I felt like such a failure. I started to clean up my mess but I couldn't help the fear that I had, that Sam would get himself in such a state that he would again be brought home by the police, I knew that would be my fault again, I simply couldn't bear going through that again, I decided to phone him.

"Fuck off" he said softly down the phone before hanging up.

Tearful I tried again, " Sam please talk to me"

"You fucking POM, you better not be home when I get there, I'll fucking kill you" his words were slurred.

Although his words frightened me I wanted him to know that I was sorry, I knew that I had done something wrong and needed him to forgive me.

"Please Sam, I'm sorry" I begged.

"Fuck off, you better make sure that the house is clean when I get home"

"I'm trying" I stammered

"Yeah that's the fucking problem"

"Where are you? Please come home" I begged him

"Fuck off" he shouted before hanging up.

I tried to phone him again but the phone just rang, so I tried again and again and again but still he wouldn't answer. I began to panic, I couldn't understand why he wouldn't talk to me, I'd told him how sorry I was. Yet his words were ringing round my head, "…I'll fucking kill you" I needed to hide from him. I decided to leave, I had to get away packing a bag with just enough for one night I hoped that Sam wouldn't mind. He wasn't happy with me anyway I thought he would be happy with me not being there for a couple of days. Yet even though that made sense to me I couldn't help the thought in the back of my mind that Sam would be more angry that I had left him, so I decided to try and phone him again.

"Sam, I'm going to go away for a couple of days" I said

"Where? Who the fuck with? I knew it, I knew that you're seeing someone else, you better be there when I get back, you stupid POM" he shouted down the phone before hanging up. I knew then that no matter what I didn't want to be there when he got back, it wasn't safe. I phoned for a taxi and waited impatiently outside.

I spent that night at the home of a friend of Sam's and his family on their sofa, I slept wonderfully well that night. I didn't need to worry about Sam going there to get me, there was no way that he'd go there, not that house and for once I allowed myself to speak about my worries and ask for advise, was I the one who was wrong or was it Sam.

The next morning I asked Sam's friend to take me home and to come with me to the house I was too scared to go there on my own. As we pulled up outside my house I could feel my stomach tighten into knots, his Ute was there so I knew that he had at least managed to drive it home. My hands began to shake and my heart was pounding in my chest. I knew that he would be cross I just hoped that it wouldn't last too long. Silently I put my key in the lock and turned, but the door wouldn't open more than a couple of inches.

"He's put the chain on" I whispered.

The bangs from inside grew more violent,

"I think we should go" Steve advised

"I need to talk to him" I reasoned

"Who's there" Sam shouted, through the door

"It's me" I answered

The door suddenly opened, only this time in my eye line was Sam's hand holding his crossbow.

"Fuck off or I'll kill you" he spat through the gap.

Falling back I watched stunned as Sam slammed the door shut.

"We need to go" I advised Steve

"Why? You said you wanted to talk to him" he asked puzzled.

"I know, I know but he just pointed that crossbow at me" I explained.

"What?"

"His crossbow, he's not in the mood right now to see me" I called back to him as I made my way to his car.

I watched as Steve tried the door, he seemed to share some heated words with Sam before coming back to the car.

"He'll let you in now" he gestured to the house.

"I don't want to, this is why I came to your house last night" I reasoned.

"It's alright, you'll be fine go on, go and speak to him" he said.

Gabbing my bag I breathed deeply as I slowly made my way back to the house, looking behind me I watched as Steve drove away.

"On your own again, girl" I whispered to myself.

Again I tried the front door, this time it opened fully. Glancing inside I placed my bag in the hallway, I hated times like these, I could never be sure if Sam going to leap out from somewhere. Walking through the lounge and dinning area I couldn't believe the state that he had managed to get into in just one night. The kitchen hadn't faired better, all the mess made me think that I'd probably done the right thing, otherwise instead of broken plates it could have been my broken bones.

"Sam" I called out

"Bedroom" came the answer

Breathing deeply I entered the bedroom, Sam was under the covers.

"Are you ok?" I asked

"What do you think?" he replied

"You scared me" I countered

"Come here" he gestured to the empty space beside him.

Climbing in beside him, I lay as still as I dared still waiting for the yelling to start.

"I can't believe that you didn't stay here last night......."

"You said you were going to kill me" I reasoned, if I'd stayed he would have been just as angry as he was now.

"You shouldn't have got anyone else involved, they didn't want you there, they were only doing it for me. If you ever leave this house again I'll never let you back in. You should be thankful that I had a word with Steve, but don't ever go back there again I don't want you near those people unless I'm with you." he ordered.

"But their your friends" I said, confused.

"No Steve is my friend, the rest of them are wasters" he corrected me.

I knew better than to argue, I liked them they were good people, genuine.

"I got drunk because of you, that night you spoke to the police has got me in shit, now I'm having to get myself out of it." he advised.

"But I didn't say anything" my voice was whining now.

"Shut up, I know you can't help being stupid I just can't believe that I thought that I could teach you, now go to sleep" he barked.

I didn't argue it wasn't worth it, Sam probably hadn't slept last night and it didn't matter to him that I had. He wanted me where he could keep an eye on me. Even if it meant the cleaning wouldn't get done until later, which of course would be my fault.

6

Sept 2002

The announcement came, we would soon be landing in Singapore. Checking on the in flight 'computer' I realised I still wasn't far enough away, a few inches is not enough. I'd become prone to panic attacks since me and Sam had married. I was always worried that I wouldn't do the right thing or that I'd end up at the wrong place at the wrong time and now was no exception. I couldn't help but think that being as stupid as I was that I had somehow managed to get on the wrong plane , it didn't matter to me that other people were there, going back to England I couldn't help but think that it was some kind of conspiracy and when I got onto the connecting flight it would take me directly back to Brisbane and straight into Sam's furious arms. He must know by now what's going on, or maybe he didn't and was waiting to give me a punch for worrying him. That would be right, I was always doing stupid things I never seemed to understand that he did what he did because he worried about me. He always told me that he was 'teaching' me but I hated it. Maybe he was right and I was not only stupid but ungrateful as well. I know that my mum thinks that I'm not capable of taking care of myself, that I trust others to much and always get hurt, and now I was just proving her right.

When we landed, I waited. Maybe I was waiting for Sam to turn up and take me back to Australia or maybe I was just waiting until I woke up. How could I have made this decision when I didn't even know if it was the right one? I needed Sam and he needed me, but I

46

know that we couldn't be together, after all when you can never tell if you're husband is going to kill you or just punch you, you should leave right? Or maybe I was just stupid.

"Mrs Williams, if you'd come this way please" the stewardess was back again, this time she had company in the shape of security.

"Er yes" dutifully I followed, I had forgotten that this would happen, they were there to escort me to the connecting flight, something about not having a valid passport.

Unfortunately there was no way of explaining that to the other passengers, goodness knows what they thought, but I didn't care, all I wanted was a cigarette and I couldn't have one. I was straight off the Brisbane plane, straight through the airport and then into the departures area for the connecting flight. I really needed a cigarette, stood there in the departures I searched for an area to smoke, but maybe I was being stupid again, does the Singapore airport even allow smoking.

The next plane was bigger, instead of two, three, two seating it was three, three, three and I was stuck with a window seat. There was already a couple sat down,

"Hi um, do you mind if we swap, its just that I hate having to climb over people" I asked

"Yes no problem" they smiled

I didn't want them to think that I was strange but part of me did worry that my increasingly odd behaviour would seem very strange. I couldn't help but think that they may complain about me, what if I'd frightened them that much, that they had to land the plane and then send me back to Australia. Sam always told me how people thought that I was a little strange, sometimes I thought I was myself. But I was so tired of it all.

2000

The first time that I laid eyes on the property at Mount Macedon I couldn't help but be overwhelmed by its beauty. Set on twenty-six acres of land which gently sloped down from the house you could see for miles around, so peaceful. It was a new chance for us, Sam would be happier here, he'd found the property without having to rush, the dog had all that space to rum around so he wouldn't be getting in Sam's way.

The house was beautiful, made completely from wood it stood proudly at the top of a hill over looking the paddocks and flower beds. The only problem was although being made of wood the house was picture perfect it made it impossible to keep clean on the inside. The seemingly impossible task became my task. Every day I would spend hours cleaning down the walls, cleaning down the kitchen, many evenings I would simply be to exhausted to argue. I spent so much time inside my own head I hated it when Sam was at home because he would tell me how I was failing, I knew that I was but I didn't want reminding all the time.

I hated the days that I wasn't working, those days were taken up with shopping, cleaning and cooking. I'd wake up, shower, get dressed then go shopping. This in itself I didn't mind, at least it meant that I'd get to see other people, I just hated knowing that I'd have to go home. Once back I'd start my cleaning regime, first I had to polish every table, TV, anything and everything, Then clean down all the wooden panelled walls, every wall from the lounge to the kitchen then the bathroom and then the four bedrooms. Once I'd made them presentable, I'd hover, this I hated as the vacuum cleaner was old and broken its suction was worse than useless. So instead of standing while hovering I spent hours crawling around on my hands and knees trying my hardest to get the carpets clean. Once that was done the kitchen was next, everything had to come out and all the worktops and cupboards had to be cleaned out. Once all the items were back in place, the bathroom was next on my list. I wasn't stupid, I knew that a house had to be cleaned but I just couldn't understand why it had to be cleaned so thoroughly every week. Or maybe I really was useless, other women manage a full time job, a home and children and I couldn't even keep a clean home.

Life didn't get much better, in fact it just got worse. One day 'it' appeared, I knew that he had it but I hadn't seen much of it, but there it was in his hands now.

"What are you doing with that?" I asked, a little nervous

"Just practicing" he replied

"But it's a shotgun"

"Mind what you say, haven't you finished cleaning yet?" he asked

Quietly I pretended it didn't matter, but I knew that it did, now he had the gun to hand I couldn't help the feeling that he would use it, when he was drunk, on me. The thought sent shivers through me. I didn't have to wait long to see what he would do with it, Sam seemed angry that I had seen the gun and so he started on the booze and he carried on all afternoon.

It was dark now and Sam had been drinking all afternoon. I knew he'd drunk enough when he insisted on only eating the lamb chops that I'd cooked, because the other stuff was too healthy. He ate like a pig, shovelling the meat in, while telling me how disgusting it tasted. Each word resulted in bits of meat being spat in my face. Sitting opposite him I ignored his rants, instead my thoughts drifted off to times when me and Sam were happy.

"I'm going out" Sam slurred as he dragged himself out of his chair.

"Where?" I asked concerned.

"Just out" he answered swaying past me.

I watched as he disappeared into the bedroom, only to reappear shortly afterwards with the shotgun in hand.

"What you going to do with that?" I asked eyeing the weapon.

"I might need it, now you stay here" he ordered as he strode out the front door.

Panic over took me as I waited impatiently for his return. When he was drunk he was just as capable of doing anything he was when he was sober. He was no stranger to handling weapons, but knowing still heightened my fears only further.

As two muffled bangs rang out I ran to the window, which was stupid as it was pitch black outside, only stars were available to offer some kind of light but still I searched for some movement. I couldn't help but think that Sam wouldn't return and that I'd have to go looking for him only to come across his blood soaked body. What if he had shot himself? It could have been by accident but more than likely by design, he'd often speak of wanting to die when he was pissed.

"What are you doing?" Sam yelled from the front door.

Startled I spun round, "I heard bangs" I answered .

"You should mind your own business" Sam advised as he walked towards me.

"I'm sorry", the pounding in my chest began to hurt.

"That's always you're answer, you think that saying sorry is the answer to everything, you're fucking stupid" he roared.

By now he was stood only an arms length from me. I'd never seen him so focussed before, he seemed so determined, so righteous, I didn't move. Lifting his arms Sam levelled the shotgun at my face. At that moment I knew that it didn't matter what I said or did, if Sam chose to, he could kill me right now.

"See how easy it is?" Sam asked

Nodding my head I stared straight at the monster that Sam really was. The pounding of blood in my ears was deafening , as though at any moment my skin would rip open and my blood would burst out all over the newly hovered carpet.

Teasing me Sam stood there smiling from behind the weapon, strangely enough it occurred to me that if I stuck my tongue out I'd actually be able to touch the end of it but then he'd probably fire for the hell of it. So there we stood, Sam daring me to screw up and me deciding if I wanted to die. I didn't, at least not that way, I wanted my family to be able to bury a body, instead Sam would make sure that I simply 'disappeared'

So I begged him, showed how scared I was, although that wasn't difficult with a shotgun to my face. I begged for his forgiveness, for what, I wasn't sure, but I begged all the same. I showed him that he was in charge, which he was, I explained that I knew that I was stupid.

"I'm sorry, please don't, you've taught me so much, I'm sorry" I begged.

"I know I'm always teaching you and you never seem to learn" he mused.

"I know, I'm sorry, I'm just stupid, please" I sobbed.

"Ok, ok" he laughed as he lowered the weapon.

My breathing had become shallow and rasping, but still I tried to keep everything as normal as possible. Bending to my right I collected the empty beer cans and carried them to the bin.

"I'll just wash these few bits" I informed him.

"Ok but come to bed when you're done" he laughed as he strode into the bedroom, still carrying 'it'. As I stood rinsing off the bits I realised how stupid I'd been. Sam loved me, he never meant to hurt me but sometimes I just got under his skin but if I actually did things the right way then he'd be fine. All I had to do was think about the washing up, I used to leave it until after I'd eaten and had unwound but that wasn't the right way to do things. Now I washed nearly everything before I sat down to eat and we never argue over that because that's the right way to do it.

Sept 2002

With the swiftness of birds the stewardess's danced around the cabin delivering more food. How strange it was that they seemed happy and elegant in their jobs. Trying their best to please all their guests, regardless of how foul tempered some of those guests could sometimes be. All of us packed in like animals yet demanding to be treated like Gods. When my turn same, I still couldn't bear the thought of eating, too afraid that I wouldn't be able to keep the food inside of me. I had grown so used to eating only when allowed to.

"You should try this, I'll be having some later" the silky voice informed me.

"No, really I'm fine" I smiled

She placed the tray in front of me,

"You should eat something, after all you didn't eat on the other flight did you?" she asked needlessly.

"No I didn't" I agreed

"Well then you're probably hungry" she winked at me, before her attention was drawn elsewhere.

Looking down at the tray my stomach churned not from disgust but from hunger.

Carefully I pulled back the cover and allowed the smells to swirl around me, 'god I'm hungry' I mumbled.

I dreaded being home or being at work no matter where I was, I was always up to no good. The only time that I was safe was when I was at home and he was being kept busy with his friends at our home. Even then I was only safe from his jealous rages for so long.

I may have been within sight of him so that he could see for himself that I wasn't sleeping around, but my actions were watched very closely. If I so much as 'invited' his friends to look at me I was whore, asking them to touch me. Blind with rage at the embarrassment that I'd cause him and his friends. He'd push me out of view. I learnt never to question him with either words or my body language. It was easier to let him push and pull me into the bedroom because on those occasions that's all it would be. A man should never hit his wife, Sam made sure that his friends knew where he stood on that point, life is all about appearances. Slowly I manoeuvred a fork full of food into my mouth, anticipating the taste, anything had to be better than the food I tried to cook in vain.

2000

"You can't even cook, I'm sick of your fucking crap food, what do I have to do to teach you, you stupid pom" Sam yelled.

I wanted to cry, to throw things to tell him to get out of my face, to hurt him like he hurt me, but I couldn't. He was right I couldn't even cook the simplest foods such as poached eggs. They had become the bain of my existence, every weekend Sam wanted poached eggs and every weekend I always got them wrong. Although Sam nearly always ate what was put in front of him, that never stopped the cries of disgust and shame that his wife couldn't even cook a steak just the way he liked it.

"Are you listening to me?" Sam yelled from behind me.

"Yes" I answered.

"Well it doesn't look like it, what the hell are you doing with that steak?" he asked slightly bemused.

"I'm cooking" I stupidly answered.

"No you're messing up" he countered.

Standing behind me he took hold of both my wrists, holding tightly he started to show me the best way to turn the meat.

"Please, you're hurting me" I croaked

Letting go, he shoved me out of the way with his body. Shocked but not really surprised I waited for him to instruct me as to what to do next. I'd been in this position with him before and had learnt if nothing else to wait for instruction on what he wanted me to do.

"Get here and actually look and listen to what I'm doing, I'm sick of eating your crap so you better learn fast" he barked.

"I'm coming" and so I stood and watched, making sure that I was far enough away from him that I wouldn't be in the firing line but close enough that he wouldn't keep yelling. Watching him take over the pounding in my head grew, I was in line for a long drawn out headache.

"Right, well I've done my best with the steaks although there wasn't a lot I could do to save them after you've had you're hands on them, now finish off" Sam passed the tongs back to me.

Shaking I took them, I hated this part, making sure that I didn't anger him anymore than I already had done. This was never easy, by this stage I was usually a wreck but I knew never to cry. Crying means that you're upset, but I had no reason to be upset. He didn't understand that what he did hurt me, he was after all teaching me to be a better wife. He is the teacher, I'm his student and crying is a weakness. A way for a women to get what she wants from a man too weak and stupid to understand a man's place verses a women's place. Never show weakness or fear especially where there is no reason to do so. He is my husband, who only wants what is best for me, to help me to be a better person, a better wife.

I always made sure of what I said about my job and those that I worked with. I spent a great deal of mental energy, making sure to keep the right balance. To never talk about those that I worked with, with any sort of affection because that meant that if I wasn't already sleeping with them I must want to. Yet I had to make sure that I did mention them in a business like way, otherwise Sam would think that I was hiding something and with the way he thought of me I had to be hiding a dirty sex secret. By now I had a job I really enjoyed, it was fun. The people were nice and the money good, with prospects. None of this mattered to Sam all he cared about was how much money he'd have to spend, it didn't matter that my wage was supporting us both it still wasn't good enough. I managed for the time being to persuade him that I was fine there, but I'd keep a look out for another job. Yet I hated that, why should I look for something better when at the end of the day it would never be good enough for him. Sam would spend all the money that I'd earnt on booze, leaving nothing for me and then yell at me because I wasn't earning enough. I could never get him to understand the problem with that.

All that I wanted was a razor of my own, but we never had the money to buy me one. I always had to wait until Sam had shaved and then he would let me use his used shaver. At first I tried not to worry about it but as time went on I couldn't understand why I wasn't allowed my own razor? What was wrong with wanting to shave my legs? I soon found my answer when I asked him, he was so angry. All he could see was me wanting to shave in order to seduce other men. I wanted my own razor for myself no one else.

7

I hated the way Sam screamed in my ear when I had to drive anywhere I was still learning to drive and instead of helping me to learn all he would do was scream in my ear. Its true what they say, never get a family member to teach you to drive unless of course you favoured arguments, I didn't. I wanted to learn how to drive but we never had any spare money to do so. I had in the past calculated how much it would cost and we could do it, if Sam would just cut down on the beer. Sam at first didn't like the idea, but I begged him explaining how I constantly worried about getting pulled over. You see even though I didn't have a full licence I still had chores to do for Sam and that usually meant driving on my own. If I didn't do it I'd suffer at his hand, far worse than I would from the police. Yet still Sam refused, I had to keep begging. By the time Sam agreed it had become his idea, as he explained to me it wasn't good for me to be driving around without a full licence. I could have screamed, but really it didn't matter how the decision was reached, all that mattered was the right decision was made. In order to save money Sam took me for my first lessons, those times were humiliating, driving only worried me when Sam was around, he seemed to heighten my fears. Still he insisted on yelling and screaming, the words would bounce around the cabin and vibrate straight through my head. When we weren't on the roads I had to spend hours driving around the paddocks, carefully following the tracks that Sam had laid down for me. Yet it didn't matter how well I did it, it was never good enough. I begged him to let me have lessons, but as he said I was just ungrateful. Other people would die for the opportunities that I'd been given and it hurt me to admit he was right.

Eventually he deemed me ready to start having a few lessons, I think that he was sick of me begging. I started out with a male instructor which was a mistake, my licence almost died before I had a chance to take the test. By this time though Sam wasn't going to give in that easy, I was going to pass my test even if it killed me. So my lessons started again in earnest, this time with a female instructor and before long I was deemed ready to take the test. The theory I passed with ease and on the day of the test I felt ready. With Sam's cloaked threats swimming around my head, I set off. I wished I'd never got out of bed that day.

I'd only been in the test ten minutes when I was asked to turn into a quiet street and pull over, so far so good.

"Right I'd like you to do a three-point turn now" the tester stated.

Taking hold of the wheel I took a deep breath and began, when I was half way through the manoeuvre, I didn't mount the curb or do anything wrong. Instead a man came running out of his house, jumped straight into his car and reversed straight into me, he never even looked. It could have been quite funny, how many people do you know that have crashed when taking their test. It wasn't funny to me because as soon as the car hit, I knew that Sam would be angry that I'd messed up again. As I watched my instructor and tester trying to sort it out I burst into tears, I couldn't believe it, Sam was never going to believe me.

The test was over, I hadn't failed, it hadn't been my fault but still I wasn't allowed to continue. My instructor promised to explain all to Sam, although she seemed puzzled that he wouldn't believe me. She didn't understand, but I knew what Sam's reaction was likely to be and at least while she was explaining it would take the pressure off me. Sam took it rather well but he couldn't really argue with the damage to the car. He was probably thankful that he wasn't being charged for the repair work. A couple of weeks after that event I passed with flying colours, thankfully.

The constant need for cleaning was starting to drive me insane. I hated what I had become, always having to check and double check everything that I had done. At least though I'd learnt how to do things the right way, before having to be told to do them. This seemed to please Sam, I felt as though I was finally making him proud of me. Yet just as I felt like I was getting on top of things Sam was there to make sure I never missed a bit. I hated Saturday mornings, funnily though he only ever bothered me on Saturday mornings if he hadn't been drinking the night before. It seemed unfair that I spent so much energy trying to stop him from getting drunk, only for him then to yell and push me around the following morning. It was better when he was dead to the world in bed, it would mean the night before would have been hell but at least I'd get a few hours to myself even if they were spent cleaning. Those hours were special to me, I was able to watch my favourite program just as long as the sound was off on the subtitles were on. On the couple of times that Sam had caught me he was spitting, how could I relax when I had work to do? Even though I hated cleaning the wooden walls I always left that bit for when the program was on that way I could watch and clean at the same time. I loved watching the heroine, she was clever, powerful and beautiful all the things that I was not.

I could barely look at myself in the mirror. I was ugly, stupid and fat, I can't cook, clean or even shag the way Sam wanted me to. I tried time and again to be a proper woman but my failures only served to anger me. How I hated being what I was, sub-human was never how I saw myself when I was younger and even more stupid than I am now.

I loved Sam very much and stupidly wanted things to be right between us he was a good man. A special man, he would have made a good father given half the chance he would have made a fantastic father. One of the reasons he was how he was, was because he hadn't been given a chance to prove himself, his family had stolen his life from him, the women he had chosen in his life had stolen the opportunity to be a good father from him. I wanted our family to be complete for it to be perfect, when I asked him for the umpteenth time about starting a family I expected the same response as he had given me before, I hadn't expected him to say yes.

"Do you mean it?" I didn't dare hope, maybe this would help us, he'd have to believe me now that he know that I wanted his baby and no one else's

"Of cause I do" he grinned at me in a way that made my heart melt.

"When? In a few months?" I asked excitedly as I started to pace round the room.

"Why not right now?" he smiled as he held out his arms

"Thank you, thank you so much" I rushed to him, allowing his warmth to wash over me, I couldn't believe it, we were finally going to have the complete family that we both longed for.

Casually he moved away from me and moved into the kitchen,

"I think that you should stop taking the pill as of now"

"Now?" I couldn't believe my ears,

"Don't be stupid otherwise I might change my mind"

"Oh yes sorry" quickly I moved out of his way, no point in upsetting him now, moving into the

bedroom I grabbed the laundry 'got to keep him happy'.

Within a few weeks I'd bought a double pregnancy kit, Sam kept telling me that it was too early but I didn't care I was floating on air. Things were better between us, he was helping me around the house, he actually seemed happier, he was still drinking but he didn't scare me any more. The first test showed as negative, I think it was safe to say that I really had done that too early but there was no holding me back, I hadn't realised how important having a child had become to me. I hadn't realised how much pressure I put on the child to make everything between me and my husband alright again. I should never have done that to myself, or my child.

I decided to hold back on doing the second test, I had no doubt that I would become pregnant I just didn't know when that was going to happen and I couldn't face the disappointment of another negative result, so I waited. I only waited a couple more weeks until one morning when I was getting ready for work, I stood in the bathroom staring at the test, weighing up in my own mind whether or not to proceed, eventually convincing myself that it really wouldn't hurt to give it a go, if I wasn't pregnant yet, I would be before long.

I could feel my heart pounding in my chest, hear the blood in my ears, my hands were shaking as I placed the test onto the flat surface of the windowsill. I know it was silly to be as excited as I was, I didn't really understand why I was so excited but I was. Standing up I braced myself for only one blue line, no harm done if there was only one blue line we can keep on trying, turning around I grabbed the test. Looking down onto the test I almost swallowed my words, there was most certainly more than one blue line, falling back down onto the toilet I looked at the stick for a closer inspection.

"One, two" I mumbled out loud tracing the lines with my hands.

I could feel the smile on my face spreading from ear to ear, I was going to have a baby I wanted to scream with joy. Rushing into the bedroom I jumped on top of Sam with my legs either side of his body.

"What are you doing?" he mumbled

"I did another test" smiling at him I wanted him to guess.

"You shouldn't have done that, it's a waste of money, we won't know yet if you are or not, now we'll have to spend more money on another one, can't you do anything right?" his voice had grown dark, pushing me off, he moved to get out of bed.

"Sam", grabbing his arm I needed him to realise it was ok, "Sam I'm pregnant!"

8

Sam had decided that we needed one last adult holiday before the child put a stop to him having any fun. In the few weeks that we had found out that I was pregnant, life between us hadn't changed in the way that I had expected. He looked at me differently, he stopped yelling that was true, but there was something more sinister in the way that he looked at me. I was even sure once that I'd heard him say that he didn't know how I'd become pregnant, and that we hadn't even discussed it! I think it was then that I realised I might be in a bigger mess than I first thought. It was dawning on me that Sam either wanted to confuse me, or he really had no memory of what we had discussed.

He had decided that we would go to Surfer's paradise for Christmas and New Year, a friend and his family were going and Sam couldn't resist any excuse for being drunk. So it was decided that we would go and that we would enjoy ourselves. Travelling up there in the car, Sam was his charming self showing me his gorgeous land, allowing me to see Sydney, Sam hadn't wanted to bother, he hated the idea of what Sydney stood for, well that depended on how drunk he was. Sometimes he would tell you that it was the certain people who had 'issues' with his family, but I guess I just got used to blocking that stuff out of my mind. I concentrated on the fact that Sam was doing something for me and hadn't had to beg him to do so.

When we arrived in Surfers it turned out that all the careful planning that Sam had done still didn't work, there wasn't anything wrong with the hotel that Sam had booked us in, it was cheap and cheerful, perfectly doable for two weeks. In the end it took the whole day for Sam to refuse the hotel, and then chase down somewhere else for us to stay, the result was an apartment that we simply didn't have the money for. Which of course was my problem as I didn't earn enough and then had got myself pregnant, without his blessing. Those words stung in my ears as Sam left the apartment to find his friends, although he said he wouldn't be long I knew that was the last I'd see of him for the night. That evening I sat in the apartment with a drink in one hand while I stroked my baby, I had to let him know that I loved him and that I was sorry I was bringing him into this nightmare.

The following morning we meet up with his friends and took a walk around Surfers, it really is a beautiful place. Although all that Sam could say was how many Asians there were compared to what it was like when he was a boy. He grumbled about how he hadn't wanted to come and that he'd done it only for me, but while he was there he was going to make the most of it! Back at the apartment he told me to sit, he had something important for me to understand. I did as I was told, Sam's mod had grown dark ever since we'd found out I was pregnant, I didn't want anything to set him off. As he opened his fourth beer of the morning, the muscles in his neck tightened.

"Paul's coming up tomorrow he's going to spend the rest of the holiday with us" he turned towards me, his eyes had become as cold as stone. I knew than I wouldn't be permitted to hold his gaze,

"Ok" I whispered, surely he wouldn't hurt me, I was carrying his child, yet I knew that look, quickly I turned to examine the floor, the hairs on my neck began to stand up.

"Just so you understand", he began to move closer until he stood over me, "I'm on holiday, it will be the last holiday that I'll get the chance to enjoy because of you. Are you listening to me?"

Before I had a chance to tell him I understood, his hand was around my neck, forcing me to look at him.

"I won't hurt you, he whispered, I've never hurt you have I?"

His hand became tighter,

"No sorry" I whispered back

"All I've ever tried to do is teach you, you were nothing when I meet you"

Too late, I was an idiot, I couldn't stop the flash of anger as it ran across my face, god I was an idiot.

For as soon as he saw it, he dropped his beer and grabbed my hair.

"Don't you dare look at me like I'm a piece of shit, you were nothing when I met you." Pulling me off the settee by my hair he slammed me to the floor, kneeling over me he held me down by my throat.

"Please don't, the baby" I begged, why was I so stupid?

"Fuck you, you bitch, he sat on my chest, I've done everything for you" grabbing hold of my shoulders he lifted me forward only to slam me back down on the floor.

"I've had enough of fucking teaching you everything, you're nothing without me, again he slammed me into the floor, you're nothing but a fat, ugly, stupid fucking POM" with one massive effort he pulled me forward only again to smash me back onto the floor.

With my eyes closed, I laid there not moving, hoping that he would get bored soon. I didn't have to wait long to feel his weight move off my chest and to hear him stride into the kitchen. The fridge door opened followed by the sound of another can being opened.

"Get up" he muttered.

Now was not the time to argue, now was simply the time to do as I was told, opening my eyes I slowly got tot my knees, studying the floor as I went.

"Come on baby", Sam moved towards me again helping me to my feet gently, he took my face in his hand, "I love you but sometimes you're just so difficult. You know that I've been looking forward to this holiday yet you seem keen on making it shit. Now what I was trying to tell you before you decided to be silly, was that Paul is coming to stay with us here for a few days, then just after New Year's we're going up to Noosa, I know how much you love Noosa, it was meant as a surprise but look what you've done. Now I'm going out, you tidy yourself up and wait for me" leaning forward he kissed me gently on the lips before grabbing his beer and walking out. I was an idiot, I knew what he was like and yet I still pushed him every time.

The following morning I found him on the balcony, he knew how much I hated heights but still he insisted that I brought out my camera so he could take a picture of me posing there.

"Paul's arriving today, I'll meet him for some drinks, why don't you go shopping, the walk will do you some good" Silently I nodded and waited for him to leave, he was happier today even letting me spend some money was a good sign that he'd calm down enough to leave me alone for a while. Following his directions I made my way to the shopping complex, turned out it wasn't five minutes down the road, try more like 45 minutes, not good in forty degree heat, let alone when you're pregnant and you're husband's decided you're only good enough for the floor. Still I made it and I was determined to make the most of my free day to buy Christmas presents. I had for so long wanted to buy Sam a gold and diamond ring but when ever I mentioned it, he always told me that if I was ever going to do anything like that then he knew someone who could sell me one cheap.

"No use in paying retail" he'd always say.

Why was I so stupid? I wanted to get him the perfect gift that he didn't know anything about, something that would show him how much I loved him. So I did, $700.00 worth but the ring was perfect for him, I thought he'd love it, I bought clothes, aftershave, trainers. I felt good, sure that Sam would love all his presents. I put aside the pains in my stomach and tried to think about how happy he would be Christmas morning, I desperately wanted him to have the perfect Christmas day after all the horrid stories he told me of his family Christmas's, I wanted him to be happy. The walk back to the apartment took longer, my legs were aching and the pains in my stomach were knotting into one. By the time I made it back he was with Paul. He seemed relaxed, but I guessed that had more to do with the beer that he was holding.

The pair of them had decided they were going to rent a couple of scooters and chase around on them together, but they needed me to help them, you see you have to have a licence to rent the mopeds! I was so scared ,I hated the idea of two wheels while I was pregnant, but still Sam insisted, so reluctantly I followed them to the hire place, shaking I handed over my licence.

"I can't do this" I whispered to Sam

Taking hold of my arm he dragged me outside, "I've already told you don't spoil my holiday"

"I'm sorry" I muttered

The moment came and I had to drive the moped back to the apartment for Paul, I was petrified. My body shaking, I prayed that the hire place wouldn't let us take the scooters but it wasn't going to be my lucky day. Instead I had to take one back to the apartment to keep Sam happy, make sure that his holiday wasn't spoiled, regardless of how I felt. With no training I had no idea what I was doing. I drove the scooter down the road, I didn't know how to stop so I didn't. Instead I joined the heavy flow of traffic, following it back to the apartment block.

"I never want to do that again" my whole body was shaking as I handed the key to Sam.

Without saying a word he took the keys from my out stretched hand before missing me with his eyes. I had done what he had wanted and now he wasn't interested in me but I didn't mind at least now I wouldn't have to drive the dam thing I had a baby to worry about, Sam disappeared for the rest of the day.

As the days went by the pain in my stomach grew more intense but still Sam wasn't interested, after all none of the women who had his children had any problems. So if I was, then how could he be sure that it wasn't his kid, I hated him with a passion. So I carried on staying in or around the apartment and Sam carried on drinking. The pain became too much, I could barely move from the settee but I tried not to worry, I was sure that I'd heard somewhere that if you were miscarrying there is little or no pain, I didn't really believe it but I needed to, to deal with it. I phoned my friend who was holidaying in Surfers too and asked her to take me to the hospital she arrived within minutes.

"Where's Sam?" she asked as I climbed into her car.

"Take a guess" I replied

"Have you tried calling him?" she asked, pulling away

"He won't answer the phone" I sighed

"Sounds about right, well lets get you sorted out, we'll contact him when we can" she smiled. The journey only lasted a few minutes and soon we were outside the casualty department.

"How can I help you" the lady behind the desk asked

"I'm pregnant, but I've been bleeding for a few days" I answered, my voice barley audible.

"Ok well we'll have to take some details from you" she responded, no ounce of emotion in her voice. I stood there answering her questions without really hearing them, tiredness was sweeping across me. Soon enough I was called into a side room where a doctor asked yet more questions, before sending me out to the waiting room. Sat in silence we waited for my turn watching others go before me. My mind became clouded, my head seemed to heavy for me to hold upright, the words from my friend seemed distant, my skin didn't seemed to belong to me, but still time passed.

"Are you alright?"

"Huh" I mumbled

"Stay there"

Turning my head was hard work but I followed my friends legs as she marched up to the desk, before I closed my eyes.

"Hi wake up"

I could feel my shoulders moving but my head seemed independent from my body, but I opened my eyes and smiled to my friend, she looked worried.

"What's happening?" I asked her, but my words seemed to belong to someone else.

"You didn't seem to be with me then honey" her voice, distant

"I feel tired that's all" I tried to reassure her.

Still we waited, I was getting angry now, I'd been waiting two hours, sat on a plastic chair, knowing that the more time I was there the greater chance that Sam would be angry.

"Mrs Williams?" A nurse had appeared from one of the doors to my right.

Slowly I got up and made my way into the room, after explaining why I was there I sat down on the bed while the nurse went to get the doctor. With my friend beside me I allowed myself to relax a little, after all I was in the best possible place. After only a moment a doctor appeared asking me questions, but I didn't really hear him, my head was heavy again, his voice was distant and my words seemed jumbled.

"Please help my baby"... ....

A sharp pain brought me back to the room and to the noise of the staff around me.

"Ouch"

"Mrs Williams can you hear me?" the male doctor seemed to be talking clearer.

"Mmm" I smiled, it was nice to see someone worried about me for a change.

The doctor disappeared from my view, and there my friend stood although now she didn't seem to be hiding her worry.

"Don't do that again" she warned.

"What, what happened?" I asked slightly bemused .

"You went... you're eyes....you left us" she seemed confused.

"How long for?" I was surprised at myself, it didn't worry me, it actually interested me.

"Long enough"

"Right, I'm going to take your blood pressure and take a look at what's been going on" the doctor had returned.

After he took a few tests, we were taken up for a scan. Lying there I was terrified but exhilarated, I was going to see my baby for the first time. Although I was told that with all the bleeding that my baby could have died and that it was still possible that the baby could, but I tried to block those thoughts out of my head. Lying there I waited, the jelly was put on my abdomen and the machine flickered to life. I watched the screen waiting to be told that everything was ok but before they had a chance I saw my baby move on the screen before me. My baby was still with me that was all I needed to know.

"Is everything ok?" I asked

"I'm not the doctor, I'm the technician"

"Just tell me is my baby ok?" I asked

The technician stalled for a moment before answering

"You're baby's still with you" he replied.

That was all I needed to know.

I didn't want to explain myself, the way that I was acting to some stranger, all that I needed to know was that my baby was ok, and that I didn't need to worry Sam over nothing, after all he always told me I was stupid and I didn't want to give him another example of me being stupid. They wanted me to wait for the doctor but I knew deep down what the doctor would say and I didn't want to hear that I had failed in being a mum so I left.

9

Sam had been furious with me for involving his friends wife in what he called my parlour games. After teaching me the error of my ways, he demanded I stopped with my stupidity and never speak of the bleeding again. I had managed to spoil the first half of his holiday and he didn't want me ruining our stay in Noosa. Making our way up to Noosa was horrific, by now I knew that there was something seriously wrong but Sam wouldn't allow me to discuss it. He just wouldn't talk to me about it. We stopped off once for petrol and I hurried to the toilet, I had to check myself, surely no one bleeds this much! Sat down on the toilet I looked down between my legs to see continually scarlet red blood leaving my body. I knew I'd lost my baby, but I hoped that I was wrong, needed to speak to Sam, but I didn't dare discuss it with him. I knew what he thought about my stupid whinging besides he had told me that if I did lose the baby that would just prove that it wasn't his, because none of his other girlfriends miscarried. God I hated him. We made a stop over at one of Sam's friends place, I was under strict instruction not to mention anything about the pregnancy or the bleeding. Yet all I wanted was for Sam to speak to me, I couldn't keep on losing this much blood even a stupid POM like me understood that.

Sam had decided on camping in Noosa, only on the second day when the pain was so extreme did I find the courage to speak with him. I had stumbled into the shower block to check on the blood loss, it had slowed down a great deal but my stomach had bloomed I really looked like I was full term, which scared me a great deal. I was in a huge amount of pain, I'd lost a great deal of blood I knew that I must do something about it. I wanted him to see the pain that I was in, I needed him but I knew unless I shocked him into realising what was happening he never would be there for me.

Watching him sort out the tent I took a deep breath,

"Sam please come with me and have a look at how much I'm bleeding" I asked.

"Fuck off you fucking dirty bitch" he seethed.

Shocked I sat there, I hadn't wanted to scare him I just needed him to see what I was seeing.

"Please there's something wrong" I whined

It didn't matter though, he wasn't interested , sometimes it was so easy to hate him.

I sat numbly watching him put the tent together himself, ignoring his moans about putting it together by himself. It didn't matter anymore that he wasn't interested in trying to save our baby's life even though I was. So I ignored his moans to help, all that I wanted was my baby to be safe. I had wanted a baby for so long, I had talked to god and begged for his forgiveness for my terrible sins, I hoped that it was true that I wouldn't be judged by him until I passed, until I had a chance to make things right, I hoped and prayed that god wouldn't punish me. I wanted and loved my babies and now I was in a fight to save the one that was growing inside of me.

After a while Sam grew tried of me being miserable, why didn't I have the strength to say no? but I needed him with me I wanted Sam and I wanted my baby, my head hurt so much. Yet still I knew that what Sam wanted he got ,if he didn't get what he believed was his then god help anyone in his way. I knew that by doing what Sam wanted I was hurting any chance my child had , but I was so scared, I didn't want to die. I just wanted a chance to prove to just one person that I was worth the air that I breathed so I chose my own physical well being over that of my baby's who was surely dying inside of me. May god have mercy on me. Sam went shopping alone.

"Stay here I won't be long" he said

"What am I suppose to do?" I asked

"Sunbathe" he replied

"What?"

"Sunbathe, the least you could do while you're pregnant is try and look good"

"Ok" I mumbled

I watched as Sam got himself ready to leave he didn't have a care in the world.

"Follow me" he suddenly called.

Looking up I saw him start to walk away, quickly I followed, when we came to a stop I found myself on the beach.

"Stay here until I come back" he ordered

"How long will you be?" I asked, a little scared that he was leaving me on my own, surly by now he realised the state that I was in.

"As long as it takes" he replied

So I watched him as he walked away from me, never before had I felt so alone. All that I wanted to do was rest, I needed to stay calm, to relax, but how could I? He had told me to stay where I was, he would know if I had wondered away even for a moment, why was I so weak? I hated myself, maybe my baby would have stood a chance had I been strong enough to stand up to Sam. Yet maybe who ever God was, he was right about me, what kind of mother would I make if I couldn't even defend my baby against his father. I cried as I laid down on the sand, I knew that I shouldn't be there, it was way too hot for someone in my position to be in and yet I couldn't move I didn't want Sam to hurt me but I didn't want my baby to die, I was lost.

When Sam returned five hours later I hadn't moved from my place just like he told me, I wasn't stupid. He was so full of life, yet all I wanted was a cuddle from him, some sort of sign that he knew the pain that I was in, but I got nothing.

"Lets go canoeing" is all that he sad.

Me being so stupid and weak I agreed, by then I knew that my life was over, I had nothing left inside to give anyone. I followed him like a lost sheep as he collected the canoe, yearning for him to hold me, to tell me that everything was going to be ok, he didn't.

By now I had almost given up hope of Sam actually listening to what I was saying, he didn't seem to care that I was bleeding, that our baby was dying for all we knew our baby could already be dead and he couldn't give a rats arse about any of it. I was dead inside I knew what was happening and I was utterly powerless to do anything about it. Sam told me we were to visit Paul and so off we went. I almost smiled to myself because I had a good idea that Paul really wasn't interested in seeing us, he seemed to be trying really hard to avoid us but you couldn't blame him, after all I was having a miscarriage and Sam was refusing to acknowledge me, that would be enough for anyone. As they chatted in his motel room, I felt a whoosh like I hadn't felt before and ran into the bathroom where I quickly sat down on the toilet. I knew that now was the time.

"Sam....SAM........SAM" I shouted so loud I thought my throat would rip apart. Looking down between my legs I just stared in horror at all the blood.

"WHAT" he shouted back through the closed but unlocked door.

I know that tone in his voice, he was pissed off but I didn't give a dam.

"SAM get in here NOW" I screamed , the blood wasn't stopping.

Slamming the door into the wall he marched over to me.

"What the fuck is wrong with you?" he demanded

"Sam have fucking look for yourself" I yelled back at him. I had to yell, I had to make him understand what was happening.

Looking down at me he looked between my legs and finally I could see the realisation on his face. The bastard finally believed me.

"Is this what its been like?" he asked his voice strangely quiet.

"It's been bad but not this bad I need to go to hospital" the tears were gliding down my cheeks.

"OK" he whispered, turning his back on me he steadied himself on the wall before walking away from me.

Cleaning up the best that I could I followed him outside. The sky was the clearest blue I'd ever seen, baby boy blue.

"Lets go" I said, climbing into the cabin of the Ute, from the corner of my eye I watched as Sam and Paul continued to talk as though this was the most normal situation they'd found themselves in. Impatiently I lent across the cabin and slammed the horn.

"I'm coming" Sam shouted before turning his attention back to Paul.

Minutes later he climbed into the drivers seat and put the Ute into gear, backing out of the car park we drove in silence. The only noise that bridged the void between us was my breathing, the pain was intense. Grabbing hold of the door handle I squeezed it until my nails pierced the tender skin of my palm.

"There's a hospital just up here" Sam broke the silence, only no emotion came with it, biting my bottom lip I nodded.

Pulling up to the entrance of the hospital Sam jumped out, slamming the door as he went. Only then did the pain stop and only then did I know for sure in that moment I knew, my life was gone.

"Come on" Sam had opened my door

"I can't, I can't move" I yelled at him.

"Come on" he insisted

"For fucks sake I can't fucking move" I yelled back

It seemed funny that for once I was in control, he didn't question me, didn't tell me that I was being stupid he simply understood and listened to me, he actually heard what I had to say or at least what I shouted at him.

He returned a moment later with a wheelchair, my control had gone as quickly as it had appeared.

"Get into this" he ordered.

Manoeuvring myself out of the Ute was certainly more difficult than it had been getting into it, for I knew what had happened and my energy to fight had gone with it. I sat numb in the chair, allowing Sam to wheel me. With each second that passed his panic grew, I was losing a great deal of blood it was flowing everywhere, I didn't care that people were looking I didn't care that it was embarrassing to Sam.

"You have to help my wife"

Sam was talking to someone, but I didn't care, I was trying hard to keep my head straight and my eyes open.

"This is a private hospital…."

"You need to help her……can't you see all that blood….?"

Sam may have been able to control me but he still had difficulty getting others to do what he wanted. If I had more time I might have thought more about that but as it was I just wanted some help. Sam allowed the nurse to wheel me through, I was of little use to him now.

"Is that your Ute outside the front entrance?" another nurse had appeared beside Sam.

"Er yes, yes it is" Sam answered.

"You need to move it"

"Yeah whatever" Sam dismissed her with his body

"Now mate" the nurse insisted.

"Ok, ok just give me a minute" Sam snapped back

The nurse left with a knowing glance towards me.

"I'm going to have to move the Ute" Sam needlessly told me.

"Ok" I mumbled

"I might just get something to eat, I could really go for fish and chips, I won't be long" Sam gently kissed my cheek before rushing out the door.

"He isn't serious is he?" asked the nurse

"Yeah" I mumbled

"He should be here with you, not going for fish and chips, you should tell him, look do you want me to go and get him?" she asked concerned

I didn't need her judging my husband, she doesn't know him or me or what our relationship is like, I didn't need her pity.

"Leave him alone, he was only trying to lighten the mood, he didn't mean anything by it" I wanted to sound in control sure of what I was saying, but instead I sounded weak and unsure.

10

Sam did return twenty minutes later, by which time the polite conversation between me and the nurse had finished. Where he had come back from, he wouldn't say. I was sure that I could smell the faint odour of salt and vinegar seeping out of his skin. I just had no energy to query what would more likely turn out to be my imagination. The nurse amused me, she behaved as though she were able to read my mind, 'why bother questioning something if you're sure that you won't get a straight answer?' lying on the uncomfortable gurney I felt another urge to push, the pain ripping through my body. My screams seemed so distant to my ears I was only able to hear them as mine because of Sam's insistence that I shut up, after all I hadn't even asked him how he was doing. I was being selfish, blind to his pain.

What happened next remains a blur, perhaps to remember it clearly would be more than my body could bear and so my mind simply refuses to remember. More likely my inability to remember lies more with my bodies response to the blood loss, pain and fear than the worst that life has to throw at me. I vaguely remember expelling something from my body, the nurse explained that it was a blood clot, whereas my husband explained it was my baby.

The next thing that I remember is being told that I couldn't stay there, it was after all a private hospital. I'm sure that the nurse said something about organising an ambulance to transfer me, yet I can't be sure, after all my husband has always wanted the best for me so had there been an ambulance he would have wanted me to take it. Not that we could actually afford the ride anyway. It would have been selfish of me to take that money, when Sam was more than capable of driving my ungrateful shell onto the next hospital. So somehow I found myself leaving the kind nurse behind.

It had grown dark outside, the air cooler on my skin, but still my skin burned with pain. Sleep was keen to take over my limbs and I had little energy to stop the coming tide from washing over me. This time he allowed me some peace even if it was only for a little while.

I woke suddenly, the music from the radio jilted my body so severely that the pains in my stomach, legs and back escaped through me escaping in twisted moans from my dry mouth.

"Bout time you woke up" Sam bellowed, his eyes not moving from the road.

"The radios so loud" I muttered

"What?" he asked, annoyed

"Sorry" I responded, even now when I should be thinking other things I was stupid enough to criticize Sam. He was trying to help me, to help his wife but I was annoyed with him for trying to relax with the music. Sometimes I was just as stupid as Sam claimed me to be.

"There's always something going on with you, you're not capable of doing things normally god here I am on holiday and look at what you have me doing. It's late, I'm tried, I want a drink but no I have to take your lazy arse to hospital." he seethed.

"Sorry" I muttered again. I could tell from the tone of his voice that he was more annoyed with my inability to learn than he was angry.

So we sat in silence, never looking at him as I feared he thought I would be defying him if I looked at him. How long it took I couldn't say, the time passed in moments of pain intermingled with Sam's occasional swearing.

The new hospital was larger, busier and noisier than the other it, leaving me in no doubt that it was a public hospital. The staff appeared to have been expecting us as I was taken through straight away. Laid down again I grew frustrated, the smell of bleach attacked my senses, even more so when I realised that the smell was only there to cover up the smell of death. Doctors and nurses floated by me, speaking over me.

"Fix the arm …. Send him on his way" the words floated around my head.

Although my fears were acknowledged I was simply told a scan would be done to see if the baby had died. Words I never wish to hear again. Tiredness and pain washing over me my memory remains hazy, unaware of time passing I waited for my turn to come with the ultrasound. Knowing what the scan would show and actually wanting to know, remain poles apart in my thinking. Not knowing meant that I could still pretend to myself that everything would be ok, that somehow my baby was still with me.Wheeling me into the room, I knew that I could no longer hide inside my head. Sam had retreated to the door, he look as through he was simply waiting for an opportunity to flee the area. Two men were in the room, I don't know if there were doctors or nurses or what, all I remember thinking was I had no desire to remember them. They were the ones that could destroy my life. The coolness of the jelly soothed my painful belly. Turning away from Sam my eyes became glued to the screen at the front of the bed. Watching the screen flicker to life I willed the picture to become clear, for it showed only a grainy nothing. They complained that my bladder wasn't' full enough, at this rate we could be waiting for another hour.

"I can't wait anymore" my voice sounded confident, I needed to know the truth.

"We can do an internal ultrasound" came the response.

"Do it" I responded

Whatever was said next I never heard, I just needed to know. I barely heard them when they requested I bring my feet up to my bum. Normally I would be crippled with fear lying in the position they use for smear tests but I was still hoping against hope that my baby would be safe. So I tolerated the embarrassment and the pain when the internal scanner was inserted. Lying there I searched the screen for my baby, desperately my eyes darted from one part of the screen to another. It was no good, my baby was gone, pushing them away from me I scrambled for the sheet to cover my useless body. Their words drifted around me, they confirmed that my baby was gone, saying that they were sorry. Yet I knew that they didn't mean it, how could they? They wanted to operate on me.

My throat ripped open as I screamed at them to shut up and leave me alone.

"Sam where are you?" I yelled, his body appeared in front of me his eyes were empty, pools of blackness

As I was wheeled through the corridors I became aware that Sam was no longer with me. He had left at some point after we had left the scan room, but exactly when it was it didn't matter. The corridors had grown quiet and dark it was late now and tiredness was taking over my body.

"Please don't put me in a room full of pregnant women, I couldn't take that, please don't" I begged the nurse who was organising where I'd be staying on her ward.

"Sssh everyone's sleeping" her words cut into my flesh. Even so I knew she was right, I was too busy thinking of myself I had to start thinking of others, like my husband. That's why he'd left me there alone because I hadn't even thought about him, I hadn't even asked him how he was. I was pushed into a side ward and menovered to a bed to my right. With whispered orders I moved onto the bed, I watched as the two nurses left the room through the door on my left. With help from the soft light from the nurses station I was able to make out that the bed directly in front of me was empty. The bed in front but to my right was hiding a human form as was the third and final bed to my right.

I was woken early, the time isn't clear in my mind, I was woken not for breakfast but for them to operate. I didn't ask them what it involved I simply told them no, I'd had a fear of hospitals for a few years . The last time that I was put sleep against my wishes was horrendous, it still gave me nightmares. Yet here I was being told what they going to do and they wouldn't listen to me. I had no say with them, yet still what did I know, I was stupid. How or what happened next I don't know, I just couldn't stay there anymore. Arguing with the staff was getting me no where, so I left them my body while I took my mind elsewhere.

"Mrs Williams"

Startled and angry I sat up and swung in the direction of the voice. My fist quickly made contact with the chubby face of the doctor, his defences too slow to avoid my fury. I believed it to be the doctor who hadn't listened to me back on the ward. I had warned him what I was like after I'd been put to sleep, fear and panic takes over. The look on his face said it all, he hadn't believed me. The nurse on my left held me from behind while I screamed at the vile doctor, he left, instructing the nurse to stay with me until I calmed down. Shaking myself free from the nurse I turned my back on her, it wasn't as though I blamed them I have the up most respect for those trained in the medical area. A wonderfully charming friend of mine had trained in that area while in the army, he was a wonderful man I often thought about him. I was angry with these people though, why was it that some medical staff believe they are always right.

Waking, some what calmer, I realised I was again back in the side ward. The other women were awake and chatting to their visitors. This only made me realise how alone I was, Sam still had not reappeared but I wasn't surprised, selfishly I didn't want him there, I couldn't deal with his accusing eyes. Slowly I got off the bed looking down at the floor, I realised with horror that all those strangers hands had been on my body. Had I had more control over myself I would never have allowed them to touch me. Again I had failed, they had to touch me to save my life because my stupid body had failed to keep my baby safe.

"I need a shower" I told the nurse who had entered the room.

"Ok, do you need some help?" she asked

"No I can manage, I just need my stuff, I'll have to wait for my husband to get here" I informed her.

"Ok well, he's been in, he dropped off some stuff for you" the look of pity on her face was too much to bear.

"When will he be back?" I asked turning away from her

"He said he wouldn't be long, he asked about when you can leave but as I told him you'll need to speak to the doctor first….. Actually speak to him" she said, the corner of her mouth curling slightly into a knowing smile.

Taking hold of the bag that she held out to me I hobbled out of the ward and followed the signs to the shower.

Unaware of time passing I allowed the water to wash away the dirty handprints, yet no matter what I did I couldn't ease the aching in my chest. Although I allowed myself a few tears I did not allow my self many, I simply couldn't risk my eyes turning red and blotchy I couldn't allow Sam to see me weak. Climbing from the shower I turned my back to the mirror and rubbed my raw skin dry. Sam had brought me clothes that did not fit, I knew it was his way of telling me that I had put some weight on because of the baby, he couldn't possibly expect it to come off that quickly. Leaving the sanctuary of the shower room behind I pulled my t-shirt over the top of my shorts in a vain attempt to hide the fact that I couldn't fasten them. Walking back down the ward I avoided the looks of the staff, I had no strength to deal with them, I was too busy trying hard to make sure that my legs worked the way that I wanted them to.

"Hey you, lets go" Sam's voice cut through my thoughts.

Looking up I watched him stride towards me,

"I can't, I'm meant to wait for the doctor" I replied

"Well how longs that going to take?" he asked

"I don't know"I answered

Sam followed me back into the ward, looking around, the woman next to the empty bed had a different visitor to the one she'd had before. Ignoring them I climbed back onto my bed, pulling my knees up to my chin I studied my feet. Sam pulled up a chair and sat down next to me.

"Well I've been back to the campsite and packed up everything, can't believe the money I've wasted on the campsite. This holiday has been a disaster, I've phoned my uncle, we'll stay with him for a couple of days ......" Sam's voice droned on and on around my head.

"That's it, we've waited long enough lets go" Sam stood grabbing hold of my bag.

"We're meant to wait, I want to wait" I responded still not looking up from my feet.

"Lets go" he barked pulling at my arm.

Relunctly I followed his lead, my head was hurting and my body ached too much to argue. Besides he loved me, he only wanted what was best for me. So I followed him out of the ward, past the nurses station and out to the Ute.

11

We left Queensland only a couple of days after we had planned, Sam didn't want to lose any more time than we already had. I just did as I was told, too numb to query anything. Our things packed and loaded onto the Ute, our goodbyes said and still I felt nothing. I was empty, nothing, worthless my baby was gone and I had no one to hold. My body ached and my head hurt but still I said nothing. Sam I'm sure tried to speak to me but I heard nothing he had to say. Although I watched out of the window I saw nothing of what we passed but I didn't care nothing mattered to me anymore. After a while Sam flicked on the radio, I guessed he needed a distraction. So we listened to the radio in silence, only occasionally did Sam say anything, but I just wasn't interested in what he had enjoyed about his holiday. I hadn't after all, my baby was dead, or hadn't he noticed? The first notes of the track escaped from the radio and brought me back from my thoughts. Such a beautiful song, the moment I'd heard it for the very first time I loved it and when I'd realised what it was about I loved it even more. Yet no sooner had the smile spread across my face, did Sam switch it off.

"Why did you do that?" I asked him annoyed.

"I don't want to listen to it" he replied sharply

"But I love that song, I want to listen to it" I said

"Well I listened to it the night I had to leave you in the hospital it made me cry and I don't want it to upset you" he said

"Please I want to listen to it" I begged

"No" he answered

So that was it, he didn't want to listen to it because it had upset him but what about what I wanted, that didn't matter to him. Turning away from him, I leaned my head against the window and closed my eyes. Imagining back only a few weeks, I saw myself sat on my sofa at home with the music channel on. There I was stroking my stomach and singing the song to my baby. Now though I was trapped inside my body that had failed me, beside a man I despised and my baby was gone. Pretending that my baby was still with me I began to go through the song inside my head. 'With arms wide open….I'll show you everything.'

The rest of the journey seemed to melt away from my memory, I've no idea if we stayed overnight anywhere, it seemed likely that we would have done but I simply have no memory of the rest of the journey. I was only aware of emptiness that had taken over my being, why did my baby have to die? My world was gone, my body had failed me and I was useless, all that I wanted was my baby to hold and to love. Did God think that I wouldn't make a good mother? Why did my baby have to die? I loved my baby and would have treasured and cared for him until my dying day. Why was I being punished or maybe Sam had been right all along. I was useless and stupid and didn't deserve my baby, I too died the day my baby died.

Once we were back home, I still hadn't found my voice. All that I wanted was my dog, Llewellyn, he understood me even when Sam either wasn't capable or simply didn't care. He seemed only interested in me being normal, doing the housework and cooking but I wasn't interested. Still it didn't take long to demand that the housework got done. After all I hadn't gone back to work, so the housework was the least that I could do. All that I wanted was to be left alone with my thoughts and dreams of my baby. At the hospitals that I had been passed to and from, they advised me to take it easy. I'd been bleeding heavily for fourteen days and my body needed to rest. I didn't care, I only wished I'd died that day so that I wouldn't feel this emptiness. Within two days, I guess Sam was sick of me walking around in a daze or maybe he was trying to help me. It didn't matter what the reason, the housework needed to be done. So I crawled around on my hands and knees and hovered his dirty floor, I had to make sure that no one saw me, Sam didn't want anyone thinking that he was a bad guy. I did as I was told but I'd lost my heart, I felt a shadow of the person I had been. I barely noticed anything that Sam did, I wasn't interested anymore and he knew it.

Sam decided within a few weeks that we needed a change of scenery, our time was nearly up on the property anyway. Somehow it was decided we would move up to Queensland, along the coast where we'd been holidaying. For once I whole heartedly agreed, I wanted to be near my baby. I hated where I was, I had no happy memories just heartache. Yet somehow even though my baby died in Queensland, the idea of living there, of being close to my baby actually filled me with hope. I did secretly hope that at some point I could get to the hospital that had taken the scan and get a picture. Sam hadn't allowed me one at the time but I wanted to have something that I could show other people. Something that I could be proud of, to say "here's my baby". I didn't want people to see me as someone with no children, I did have, but he died.

We had to move back in with Sam's Nan, once we'd left Mount Macedon in order to save some money for the move to Queensland. I didn't mind too much at least it meant that I wasn't constantly cleaning. I did though have to behave myself in order not to offend either of them. I also learnt that in order to please Sam I had to make an attempt to at least look happy. It offended him that I walked around looking miserable, he worried that people would think that he wasn't capable of making me happy. He needn't have worried it was me that I was unhappy with, I was the one that couldn't do anything right. I was the one who couldn't cook, clean, iron, satisfy him right, I was fat and ugly but more importantly it was my body that had let me down, I had failed at the most basic task a women does.

12

It was supposed to be a new start, but really that was a joke we couldn't even make the trip from Melbourne to Caloundra without taunts. I had somehow managed to persuade him that I could drive the Ute, after all I need a good car because my driving really wasn't that good and so he agreed I would drive the Ute which would compensate for my poor driving and Sam would drive the car that had no tax and always felt like it was going to fall apart because he was a good driver and could handle it. I felt bad for leaving my dog behind I worried that Sam wouldn't go back and get him like he said that he would, I missed my dog, he understood me.

After one day of travelling it happened, Sam was furious with me, the car he had to drive kept breaking down and that was my fault, I hated that car. We had to pull over onto the side of the road because of that dam car. It had started to smoke, that was my fault. I must have been mistreating the car before Sam had a chance to drive it. Jumping out of the Ute, Sam was yelling at me to get off the road, to get his tools, to go over to him. I could feel my head starting to spin, I hated this, we were in the middle of no where, he could kill me now and no one would ever find me. Typical stories that you hear about silly British pack packers who disappear in the Australian Outback, no one would ever question it, it happened all the time. Swallowing the lump that developed in my throat I ran back to the Ute and grabbed his tools.

"What the hell took you so long?" he said as he snatched the tools out of my hand.

The smoke had started to pour from under the bonnet,

"Careful" I whispered

"I know what I'm doing" he huffed lifting up the bonnet, he went straight to the radiator cap.

"Do you want a towel or something?" I asked

"I've got one, don't you think I have brains or something" he muttered. Walking around to the drivers door he reached in and grabbed the towel, strutting back to the engine. He wasn't thinking when he undid the radiator cap and before he had any time to react the boiling water and steam exploded from within.

"Fuck, fuck, look what you made me fucking do, you fuck"

Again it was my fault, it was always my fault maybe I hadn't been clear enough when I'd mentioned using a towel.

"Well don't just stand there you stupid POM get here and help me" he roared

Moving quickly I tried to help him, but stupid me I was being clumsy again. I always seemed to develop butter fingers when I was supposed to be being helpful. I dropped the radiator cap onto the ground it was still burning hot from the steam bending down again to retrieve it Sam grabbed hold of my hair. Knocking me off balance he pushed my face into the dirt.

"You're not worth my time, you're stupid I asked for your help didn't I?" his voice calmer now. Unable to respond to his question, I inhaled the red dust. The pain from my head signalled to my brain for my body to stay still. The more I struggled the more he had to show me who was right and therefore who was wrong. When I was still he knew then that I had learned my place. Letting go he learnt back and laughed,

"What's the dirt taste like?"

Knowing that really wasn't a question I didn't respond, just pulled my tired body up onto my aching feet. Lifting my hand I brushed the dirt from my mouth, still I didn't look at him.

"Fuck off back to the Ute, you're no good to me" he demanded.

So I did, the only thing I can do half way right was to do what I was told. I watched him struggle with the car, I knew that it was simply an overheated radiator, I even knew that not using the towel to take the cap off was a bad idea, but there was no point in saying anything, what's done is done.

After twenty minutes of throwing stuff around the road Sam was finished with the car. Putting the bonnet down, he looked straight at me, his face twisted with pain.

"That should hold" he yelled.

"How are you?" my voice timid

"It's alright" he answered.

I knew he was lying, I could see his skin was beginning to blister. Opening the door, I reached out to him. His cheek and stomach were showing the signs of being burnt by steam.

"It's fine" he insisted

"You'll need cream on those" I ignored his insistence that he was fine.

"The car should be fine until the next town" he lifted a cig to his mouth and lit it. His right hand was showing signs of being really badly burnt.

"You'll need to go to hospital"

"SHUT UP, I'm fine" he spat the words into my face.

"Cream at least, I'll go to the chemist when we get to the next town" although I knew that the burns must hurt him I couldn't help but be impressed by his ability to carry on, even if I thought it to be stupid.

13

I could hear his hurtful words as they chased me out of the house, god I hated him but most of all I hated what I had become. Moments like these made me want to die in order to be free, believing more and more that the only way to be truly free I needed to die, a small price to pay. Looking behind I watched as he charged to the front door, quickly I ran to the drivers side and jumped in.

"Give me the keys" he yelled.

Why wouldn't he leave me alone, I had to go to work otherwise I wouldn't get paid and he'd have less money to spend.

"Get out of the car, he screamed, get out before I drag you out."

I wanted to run, but where would I go. I knew that no matter what I would have to return to him at some point and he would be even more angry than at this very moment in time. Confusion clouded my thoughts, if I missed work I'd be in trouble, if I went to work I'd be in trouble. Lost.

It happened so very quickly, I saw him come round to the drivers side and open the door, but I didn't see his fist, nor did I feel it. I just remember the force knocking me sideways onto the passengers seat. Silence. My eyes began to focus on the glove box then as I moved my head, onto Sam. He stood leaning against the open drivers door, he looked exhausted he didn't look at me when he reached in for the key.

"Get out of the car" his voice carried no anger now, he reached in and pulled me into a sitting position. I slowly reached up to my face, my fingers gingerly touching my cheekbone. I saw the next one and ducked back over to the passengers side.

"I wasn't going to hit you" he seemed hurt at the idea that I might think that he would punch me again. I didn't struggle against his grip as he pulled me out of the car, I allowed him to guide me back into the house. Unable to stop myself from crying, the throbbing sensation had kicked in and my face and nose felt like they were burning.

"Sit down on the bed, he suggested, I need to get a look"

Gently he lifted my head, but I averted my gaze, I didn't want to see his eyes. If this is what his soul was like I wasn't interested in looking in the windows.

"You'll be fine, why don't you lay down and stop crying" his voice no more than a whisper now. As I turned I saw him in a way that I hadn't done before, he looked frightened.

"Don't look at me" he said as he pushed me down on the bed.

Turning away from him I faced the wall and allowed my whole body to be racked by my crying, somewhere beyond the confinement of this prison there had to be happenings. In between my sobs I could hear Sam phoning my boss and explaining that I wouldn't be there because I wasn't very well. I wondered if my boss, a kind and gentle man, could hear me crying in the background. Would he wonder why? I wondered if he knew? If he could help me? Than the guilt swept over me with another wave of sobs, my personal life had yet again affected my job, I'd let more and more people down. Sam reappeared at my side, bringing his body next to mine, his touch only made me cry harder. I lay on my side with my burning face, facing Sam, who tried to hold me but I felt numb.

"You'll have to move, I can't stand looking at it" forcefully he moved me over to his side of the bed, this time my tender face was forced onto the sheets just so he wouldn't have to look at his handy work.

My sobbing now had become uncontrollable all the months of pain had overcome me.

"I need to be sick" I spluttered

"sssh"

"I'm going to be sick" I'd found my voice and was surprised at how strong it was. Sitting up, Sam pulled me up behind him.

"You need a bath that'll calm you down and stop all this silly crying"

If its so silly, I thought, why couldn't he look me in the face.

"Come on"forcefully he pulled me off the bed and into the bathroom. Standing there, I wasn't looking as he turned on the cold water.

"It needs to be cold" he muttered to the wind

I knew there was a mirror to the right of me I needed to see my face, I wondered what was so hideous that made Sam look away. Looking at myself in the mirror I traced the outline of my nose now swollen and tender, my eye was partially closed and bruising had already started to appear, my cheek was tender and red. I watched my tears as they fell down my face, each one tracing the outline of the punch, first the bruised eye then in between my swollen nose and cheek before falling from my chin.

"Take off your clothes" Sam ordered

I turned to him, undoing my trousers, I didn't want him to see me naked, he frightened me.

"Get your clothes off" he barked.

My hands moved quicker now, I was frightened about what he would do to me if I failed to do what he said, I'd had enough fighting for one day. Hurriedly I removed all my clothes and stood there more naked than I had ever been before.

"Get in and clean yourself" he ordered. I quickly got into the bath, the cold water took my breath away. I carefully followed his lead, when he handed me the soap I washed, when he handed me the sponge I rinsed off. Soon we both sat in silence, me in the bath and Sam sat on the floor.

"Can I get out now?" I asked

"Have you finished crying" he replied

"Yes" I whispered.

"Ok" he stood up and helped me to stand, holding the towel he gently dried me. I wasn't really thinking any more all that I wanted was to hide somewhere, somewhere that only good could find me. Sam marched me back into the bed, my towel now the only thing protecting me from him. He closed the door behind him, and began to get undressed.

"Don't look at me"

I turned away, I knew what he wanted and the very idea made me feel sick. He moved towards me and took my towel from me.

"Open your legs" he barked

I began to move.

"Wider" I could hear the lust in his voice. He climbed on top of me and forced his way in, as a tear trickled down my cheek. The tear quickly made him angry, he pushed my face into the mattress, forcing his way into me I could hear his panting and groaning. Please God let it be over soon I prayed, I had not really been religious before but now I found myself praying to someone, anyone that could make me feel safe again.

"I love you, I only do what I do to help you" he groaned. My body was aching, I tried to picture myself on the beach enjoying the sunshine.

"Tell me you love me, tell me you're sorry" his thrusting was beginning to hurt but still I said nothing. Forcing my head further into the mattress he tried again.

"Tell me that you love me and that you're sorry" he demanded. And so in between mouth fulls of sheets I told him how sorry I was and that I loved him more than life its self. This for some sick, disgusting reason this turned him on even more, soon he was cuming. Rolling off me, he climbed off the bed and got dressed.

"Cover yourself up" he whispered, the disgust in his voice dripping from every word. I pulled the duvet over me and watched as he got dressed and left the room allowing a wave of relief flow over me. I didn't see him again that day.

14

We continued on in that vain, pretending to other people that we were a happy perfect couple and yet I was failing on every aspect of being a women, of being his perfect wife. As a young woman I couldn't even keep my body looking good, I'm fat and ugly my body repulses even me, not really surprising really that Sam hated looking at me, was embarrassed to be seen with me. If it was only my body that was the problem maybe I could have done something about it, but not only am I fat and ugly but stupid as well. I couldn't join in a conversation because I always said stupid things at the wrong moment, but as Sam would tell me, what did I expect after all I couldn't even spell words that a seven year old can. He wasn't being hurtful, he was right my spelling is awful and no matter how I try to better myself it never works. All I succeed in doing is making a fool of Sam. I was spoiling Sam's social life, not only couldn't he take me anywhere because of my stupidity and ugliness, he couldn't have his friends round to the house because of my inability to even keep the house clean. Such basic tasks as mopping the floor were too complicated I never seemed to be able to keep on top of all the housework that needed doing. There was sweeping the floors, washing the floors, polishing the floors but not to forget to move everything out of the way in order to do that. All the windows had to be washed, everything had to be dusted down, but of course the dusting should be done before the floors are cleaned if you didn't you would only have to clean the floors again. All the white goods had to be cleaned down, the amount of times I forgot to go outside and clean down the washing machine only showed my disrespect of my husband. The bathroom had to be scrubbed clean along with the kitchen and on and on. Every weekend these things had to be done and yet I never seemed to do them right, I was useless. Maybe I would have forgiven myself of these awful qualities that I possessed but I had no redeeming qualities, I couldn't even make love the right way, it didn't help that I was fat and ugly, after all how is Sam meant to turn me on if I don't even turn him on. Sam was right, screwing me was a chore that he wished he didn't have to perform but I'm his wife and what's a man supposed to do if his wife is as bad at the basics as I am. Teach me, I'm the student and he is the teacher.

I hated being the way that I was, not knowing how my actions were going to affect, Sam it became so tiring trying to second guess how he would react. What I hated more than anything was the 'teaching' that word sent shivers through my body, weekends were the worst. His favourite would happen if I had embarrassed him when he wasn't drunk, he would be calm, smile his beautiful smile but not say a word. I'd know though that what ever it was that I had done, it was wrong, very wrong, but Sam would wait until we got home. Calmly he would walk around the house looking for faults, it wouldn't take him long to find any, I was useless at anything to do with housework. A few times I would look him in the face when he'd start but I soon learnt that he saw that only as an act of defiance and he hated it, my only chance of it only being a 'dragging' session was to look down at the floor while I told him how sorry I was and all the ways that I was going to be a better person. As long as he believed that I had truly learnt my lesson he would only drag me around for a while.

Taking hold of me by my hair or arm which ever was easiest at the time, he would proceed to push me to the floor and drag me from room to room pointing out all the 'problem areas' with my face, yelling at me all the while. I was so stupid, I did things that upset him, when I behaved well I was treated well, when I was bad then I was punished, simple really. Yet sometimes I would yell back stand up for myself like you're supposed to, who the hell said that? Who ever it was had never meet my husband. When I was stupid to think that would actually work, stupid enough to think that he actually cared about me, the punishment was always severe. He would still push me around, pointing out everything that was wrong to me. I knew that it would either end up in the bedroom where he'd 'sniff' me just to make sure, after all why would I defend myself unless I was seeing someone else! Or we'd end up rolling around on the floor, me trying my hardest to stop him hitting me and him hitting me anyway. When ever it got that bad I knew the only way for me to live another day was to beg, to tell him how I didn't want to die. To beg his forgiveness for my stupidity, to beg him not to hurt me and as he told me, the only way he'd believe that, was for me to have sex with him like I meant it.

15

My days were taken up with worrying about what state he would be in when I got home from work. He still wasn't working we were living off my wage which was never good enough for him. All he did all day long was drink, if I was lucky he would have had far to much to start on me when I got home, but then my luck would have to hold. I must never look at him the wrong way, I must make sure that he had enough beer to see him through the night. If I was unlucky he wouldn't have drunk enough and all the things that bothered him about me would have to be sorted out there and then. I hated those nights.

On some occasions I would get home to find that he had started to cook tea, because he was sick of my crap cooking, but never the less at least it was one less thing for me to do. Those times were happy, it was like he realised that the way he had been treating me wasn't right, or maybe he just realised I was beyond help. Whatever the reason he would treat me better those nights. We would laugh, joke and if I was really lucky he would let me walk down to the beach. Yet at the same time that I would be enjoying those nights I also hated them, I knew then that I wouldn't have another night like that for weeks.

I knew that I was going to be in trouble with Sam, him and Paul were discussing something and both were furious about it but I didn't know what it was about. Swiftly Sam spun towards me his eyes were full of hatred.

"What? What's wrong?" I asked, my voice shaking. I knew that it didn't matter, what ever it was that I was supposed to have done, he was mad.

"Look what you've done to him" Sam shouted in my face

Scared I looked from him to Paul and back again.

"What are you talking about?" I asked again.

Leaning across the breakfast bar Sam grabbed hold of my hair, pulling me towards him, he tried again,

"Look at what you've done, look at Paul"

Noticing for the first time the scratches on Paul's face I understood what Sam was on about, but I still didn't understand what it had to do with me, but that didn't matter. While I was still thinking of what to say, Sam had come round to my side shouting at me for an answer.

"That was from last time, I told you!" I began to reason with him, the desperation in my voice taking over, but it was too little too late. Before I had a chance to stop him Sam had kicked me straight in the stomach, the force of which sent me of the stool. Cowering on the floor I tried to make sense of what was happening.

"You fucking POM......you disgust me.....get onto your feet or I'll kill you" his voice was calmer now, more dangerous.

Feeling for broken bones, I began to lift myself up, unsure whether that would really be a good move. Directly in front, Paul stood too ashamed to meet my gaze. I felt betrayed I had always relied on Paul to make sure that Sam wouldn't hurt me and now he was helping him, giving him a bogus reason to do it, I realised then I was truly on my own.

"Look at me bitch" Sam commanded

Turning towards Sam, I willed him to try and kill me because God helping I was going down fighting.

"I didn't scratch him" I cried

"Yes you fucking did, he's told me you did, so you fucking did" he whispered in my face, before striking me again in the stomach. The force of the punch made me double over, but I regained my composure, daring him. I hadn't done anything wrong but if he wanted me dead that was fine by me. I'd been living a death sentence since the first moment I'd met him anyway.

Grabbing hold of me Sam throw me out of the kitchen area.

"Why don't you get your stuff and fuck off, go on get out off my house" he yelled so loud I couldn't help but wonder what the neighbours must think. I had never seen Sam this angry before, not when there wasn't drink involved, he was deadly this time. Crawling along the floor I sought sanctuary in the bathroom, but Sam followed, taking hold of me by my hair he dragged me from the bathroom to the front door, where he calmly kicked me out.

"Why don't you fuck off to your boyfriends house, you'd have many to chose from" he spat at me as he slammed the door in my face.

Confused I stood there staring at the door, wondering what to do. This was a perfect chance for me to get away, he didn't want me and I didn't want him. Suddenly I noticed the shooting pain in my hand, looking down I smiled, somehow I'd managed to keep hold of my keys, now I had access to the car. Quickly I sped away from the house, I certainly shouldn't have been driving, I'd drunk too much, but I didn't know what else to do. I just pointed the car and drove, praying that Sam wouldn't follow. I knew that he would be mad as soon as he realised that I had the car, I couldn't go back now, he would kill me and there was still a part of me that didn't want to give him the satisfaction, so I drove.

Sam had told me so many times that he would kill me if I ever went to the police, that they couldn't be trusted, that they were just waiting for him to fuck up again so they'd have a chance to kill him, or lock him away and that would be my fault. People who knew my husband, who dealt with him, would never rest until I was dead, I didn't have a child of his to protect me. He was always so proud of the fact that while I remained his wife I could never be made to testify against him, he never believed that I would have the courage to, he rightly believed I enjoyed being alive too much,. Yet now I found myself outside the police station. I had no intention of telling them about what Sam did, but I needed somewhere safe to stay and they could help me. As I rung the bell I believed there would be no going back, Sam would never forgive me for this.

Having to explain to strangers why I couldn't go home was embarrassing, how do you tell someone you're afraid your husband might kill you? How do you say something like that without them thinking you're some sort of nutter or worse still, think that it was some sort of silly argument some sort of domestic that's best left alone. I told them only what I needed to in order for them to help me find somewhere to stay for the night, there was a women's refuge out of town, but that was fully booked for the night, I would have to wait until the next day, for now I would have to settle for somewhere in town. The idea filled me with dread, Sam would soon calm down enough to allow me back in. I had made a mistake, I should have waited for him to let me back in, but instead I did the one thing that he hated, I spoke to the police, to him it wouldn't matter that I had only told them about the fight and nothing about Sam himself, it would be the fact that I went to the police. But where else was I supposed to go, I couldn't go to friends because I wasn't allowed any. That night, tucked away safely in that motel room I couldn't sleep, Sam was out there and he would be mad, so very mad.

By the time daylight broke through the window I knew what I had to do, yet still I watched the rays creep across the floor. Knowing what you have to do and actually doing it can sometimes be difficult to actually put into action. Snuggling down into the bed, the warmth of the covers gently caressed every inch of my aching body. For the first time in what felt like a life time I was naked and comfortable with it, I felt no shame with my body as I lay there I was safe in my cocoon. If only I could have held onto that feeling, somehow contain it within myself and taken it with me, I would always have a smile on my face. Yet there I was being stupid again, I was, what my husband thought, an idiot someone, completely incapable of dealing with the real world. The truthfulness in which he spoke only compounded my feelings of insecurity. I had to go home, I needed him and he needed me. Bracing myself, I threw the covers from me, there was no point in waiting around, putting it off would only make the situation more difficult. Getting dressed I tried to remain calm, to enjoy the morning sunshine as it beamed through the curtains, warming my body, the glow on my face entranced me yet it wasn't going to help me. Closing the door behind me I said goodbye to the freedom that I could have had and drove towards the responsibilities of marriage that I had been so eager to run from. I had given Sam some space and time to calm down, I knew that he was going to be angry and concerned about where and who I had spent the night with but what did I expect. He loved me and all I did was throw it back in his face I had to except that my actions caused him pain I had to grow up.

Pulling into the driveway I turned the key and allowed the engine to die. Breathing deeply I focussed on my home, there was no movement and the Ute was still in the same place that it had been the night before. 'At least I know that he didn't go driving when he was drunk' I thought to myself. Walking towards the front door a noise from behind me, alerting my senses to company.

"Where the fuck have you been?" Sam's voice was low, accusing

"Motel" I answered, my back to him still

"Don't fucking lie to me, I went out earlier and I've been to all the fucking motels in Caloundra and you weren't in any of them so which fucking boyfriends did you stay at last night?" still his voice remained calm, frightening so.

"I did, I stayed at the one on the high street"

Stepping forward quickly he lifted his hand, taking hold of me neck his bony fingers dug into the tender skin of my neck. The heat from his eyes burning into the top of my head.

"Look at me" he whispered softly

Slowly I looked up at him, I loved him, wanted him to believe me but I had been expecting this, I deserved this.

"I did, I went to the police station and they put me up in the motel on the high street, but the owner wouldn't have told you that I was there because the police would have told him not to" I whispered. His fingers dug deeper into my skin, I felt weak and scared, I hated moments like these but at least I knew that these moments would come to an end.

"So why are you here now?" he asked

"Because I love you, I thought that… well maybe you'd be calmer after last night" I reasoned.

Me calmer, all I did was protect Paul and you tried to make me look like a fool you have some fucking nerve, fucking POM" discarding me he pushed me aside onto the grass.

Landing heavily on my side I lay where I was put, keeping my eyes firmly on the ground.

"I'm sorry" I whispered

"You're sorry, ha ha, you went to the police station and you're sorry, that's funny, you're best stupid comment by far"

"I didn't tell them anything I didn't give any names, they know nothing, not a thing about you, I promise I love you, I never want to hurt you, please" my voice had taken on a whining quality.

"Fuck you" he kicked the ground by my head and walked away.

Turning quickly I got to my knees, "please I'm so sorry, please"

"I knew you are, that's why I'm going to let you stay but I don't want you in the house today you can stay there where I can keep an eye on you" he smiled at me before jumping up the front steps and disappearing into the house.

Moving back onto my ankles, I allowed myself a smile he'd been a lot kinder to me than I deserved, I had caused him a lot of unnecessary pain and worry. So what if I had to wait outside until I was allowed into the house, at least I didn't get hit. My neck still hurt but at least if there were any marks from that they would disappear a lot quicker than bruises and I wouldn't have to think of another way that I'd hurt myself if anyone were to ask. In a way Sam had done me a favour, he cared about me, he loved me.

Giving Sam the money that I earned from work was the right thing to do, after all I was at work most days and because he didn't work, anything that might need paying for during the week he could pay it instead of me worrying about it. It was another way of helping me out, it showed he really loved me. It was just that sometimes it would have been nice to have a little bit for myself. I understand that with my weight problems that having money on me could sometimes be a temptation to buy junk food and undo all of Sam's good work. Sam was trying to help me, to support me, because sometimes I would go and buy a chocolate bar and that really wasn't good for me. I couldn't be trusted not to buy junk food. Yet even though I knew he did it for my own good I hated having to ask him for money for tampons. Or having to ask for petrol money then making sure that I didn't lose the receipt and the change, both of which Sam had to see. He had to know that I wasn't cheating because if I wasn't willing to look after myself why should he?

He did what he did because he loved me, yet still it pained me. I had to be careful with the money that he let me have but I also had to be careful that I was where he expected me to be, when he expected me to be there. It was no good coming home late from work, even if it was only by a couple of minutes. Sam couldn't understand why I would need to be late or early for that matter, he couldn't see that maybe sometimes the traffic was lighter than other times, instead he believed that if I was late then I must have stopped off somewhere to shag someone. After everything that Sam had done for me it only seemed fair that I was where he expected me to be. I think he believed me when I told him the truth, that I hadn't so much as looked at anyone else let alone been with them. Sam did what he did out of love for me, he had made the journey from our home to my place of work and timed it, in order to help me. He worried that those who knew that I made that journey might try and jump me, he worried about my safety, so if I was a couple of minutes late how was he too know that I wasn't lying an a ditch somewhere.

It was hard trying to explain to those that I worked with, that I couldn't stay behind after work and join them for a drink but I didn't feel comfortable doing that sort of thing anyway. Socialising with them was the least of my worries, I had already been forced to leave four jobs because of all the time I'd taken off work. After a while in a job those that I worked with would start to treat me differently, but I was stupid, I never helped myself to fit in, I expected them to do the work for me. I hated working with men, I didn't know how to talk to them. I knew that I had to be careful not to give out the wrong signals. Sam was right he couldn't help me if I gave out the wrong signals to them, I was a fool who expected others to do all the work. My concerns about what kind of mood that Sam was going to be in when I got home only made my moods at work harder to control. I so wanted to be normal just like those around me, I hated them yet I wanted to be them. Sam never wanted to talk with those that I worked with, never wanted to make the effort, why should he they weren't his friends. I didn't need any friends, I had Sam, yet still I wasn't grateful enough for that, I deserved everything that I got.

16

I knew that with each passing day I was more and more like a zombie I hated what I had become and yet I could see only one way of breaking free. The only way for this to end would be either my death or his, I wasn't bothered which that was. The only reason for not killing him was simple, I wanted to be free of him but if I finally got him back with him own medicine I would be the one going to jail and so I still wouldn't be free. I wasn't safe anywhere, let alone prison, not with his contacts. I hated him, yet he was right about one thing, I was stupid I knew what would upset him, but I'd do it anyway. I remember the look in his eyes one night. It had been a fairly good evening as good evenings in my house went. Sam was drunk as usual yet he was behaving himself. Paul was on the phone to a friend and I had just finished cleaning down the kitchen after tea. Making my way into the sunroom I looked forward to sitting down and having a drink, when Sam grabbed my arm.

"Lets have a fight, put your arms up" he ordered

"Please no, I'm tired I don't want to do this" I responded shaking my head.

Leaning forward he flicked my forehead.

"Put your arms up and defend yourself" he ordered just like in class.

Putting my arm up, I was unable to protect my face completely, my head snapped back when his fist made contact with my cheek. Looking at him through burning eyes I wished him dead.

"Defend yourself" he barked

"Please don't" I begged "please stop"

He didn't hear me, with the next punch I landed on the floor all I could think about was protecting myself the best I could, his cursing seeping into my head. I lost count of the punches but eventually he stopped and fell down onto the settee.

"Get up" he slurred

With my mind racing I picked myself up off the floor, my mouth felt wet with the bitter taste of blood.

"I'm pissed fucker, come here" he lifted his hand towards me.

I hated him but I hated myself even more, I was so weak and stupid, moving towards him I took hold of his hand and pulled him off the settee.

"I'll take you to bed" I muttered

"hmm"

Walking him through the sun room we made our way past the kitchen where Paul stood, he would have heard and seen everything from that view point. So many weak people all because of my husband, or maybe it was just me, maybe this was normal, but part of me knew that it wasn't, what scared me even more was I felt like I was losing my mind. Walking him through the house this time proved more painful than all the other nights. My frame didn't allow for 18 stone of dead weight to be carried with ease. This time I had the use of only one arm, his punches had made primary contact with my left arm resulting in it being of little use to me now. Making our way through the kitchen, where Paul stood I ignored him. My husband didn't bring out the best in people it seemed that when he was around he high lighted peoples weakness's. Letting Sam fall onto the bed I bent to lift up his legs.

"Come here" Sam whispered, grabbing my hair he pulled me towards him.

Unable to keep my balance I fell to his side. Sensing his mood I didn't try to remove his hand from me, instead I allowed him to men over me to my side of the bed. He was no threat to me now, he'd tired himself out from his earlier outburst. Now all that he wanted was to sleep and make sure that I didn't move. Little did he know that I had learnt from experiences that it would take him only a few minutes to sleep. This allowing me the opportunity to slip out from under his arm and have ten minutes to myself.

With symphonic snoring in my right ear, I knew I was safe to move. Slipping away I crept from our bedroom, through the now dark and deserted kitchen, back into the sitting room.

"Where is he?" Paul asked from the settee.

"Sssh, please he's asleep right now" I replied.

Moving towards the settee I spied my cigs, they had fallen under the coffee table. Having read my mind, Paul passed me one of his, accepting it I sat beside him. As I put it to my mouth I whimpered from the pain in my right arm.

"It's ok, let me wipe the blood away" his voice had a kinder edge to it, an edge I hadn't realised that he was capable of.

Turning towards him I couldn't be sure if this wasn't some kind of trick, if he was planning on reporting me back too Sam. I had tasted the bitter taste of blood before, but why was he deciding to help me now when before he had ignored me. When I had been bruised and damaged before he had never offered his assistance, so why now? As he wiped away my blood from my chin, I flinched.

"You're still bleeding" he whispered

Nodding, I looked away, tears of shame trickling down my chin.

"Your going to have one hell of a lump" he observed.

Taking the tissue from him, I thanked him for his help.

"How's your arm?"

The concern in his voice seemed genuine.

Yet I was still unsure , it felt like a lifetime since anyone had been interested in me.

"Sore" I responded.

"Let me see"

Turning to look at him, I had recognised the sharper edge to his voice, he wasn't asking he was demanding. Carefully I removed the outer shirt that I had been wearing, the state of my arm making what should have been a simple task painful. Sat there, my arm limp I listened to Paul's intake of breath.

"That's bad, really fucking bad"

Looking from my shoulder down to my wrist I saw what he saw, my arm was already turning black.

"Can you move your fingers?" he asked

Slowly I moved one after the other.

"Not broken" I responded

"Do you want a drink?" he asked

Suddenly acutely aware that if Sam walked in he wouldn't like what he saw, he was already far, far too paranoid about me. I knew that I would have to go bed, ignore my pain, ignore Paul's kindness for surely he would report me too Sam anyway.

"I'm going to bed" I told him.

"Are you sure? You haven't even had a smoke" reaching out he offered the fag that I had discarded.

"No, no I really must go to bed, I need to be there in case Sam wakes up"

"He won't"

"Oh he will, he'll wake up at least once tonight and god help me if I aren't there when he does"

Moving quickly I stood in the doorway.

"I won't say anything"

Ignoring him I carried on, if he was to say anything there wouldn't be anything I could say to stop him anyway. Creeping as I had done before, only this time in reverse I sneaked back into the bed under the cover of darkness.

17

I lost count of the amount of times that I would look in the mirror and see my lips swollen and split, Sam didn't need to punch me now I knew where I stood, I knew my place and yet he still would. It was only to teach me, if I got above my station, just to let me know who was in charge. In the same way we no longer made love, that had long since stopped, now he fucked my body. There was no tenderness, no care taken, no love. He would use my body when he wanted to and I would have to comply, no matter how I felt or what I wanted.

I need to find peace, I need to rest, I needed calm and yet I had no one to turn to, to share my feelings with. I was so confused as a wife, wasn't I meant to share my thoughts and fears with my husband. That never worked, if I ever complained it was always my fault and it was my fault I couldn't do anything right, I can't cook, I cant clean, I cant get a decent job, I cant even fuck properly. My head was for ever spinning, I had to be normal at work, do the job right but I must never be home any later or earlier than my husband believes to be right. I must be the perfect wife, I must never talk unless spoken too, I must never share my stupid opinions with any one. I must always make sure that the house is clean, I must always make sure that the clothes are washed and ironed perfectly. I must make sure that I do not damage anything worth any money through acts of my stupidity. I must make sure that my dog never damaged anything, which as my husband pointed out would be unlikely because the dog had more brain cells than I could ever hope to possess. I embarrassed my husband in front of everyone, I embarrassed myself, Sam hated it when it when I tried to wear pretty clothes like all the other young women, he hated the way my fat seemed to explode from my body. I hated me, I never realised before what I was, I used to pretend that I was something special but really I'm nothing. My head hurt so much, it was tiring trying to be the person that he wanted me to be. I couldn't cope some times and would yell at him but that was just me being stupid, I knew that I was burden on him. I wanted him to teach me to be a better person and yet I hated him teaching me to be a perfect wife, I just wasn't good enough. I didn't know from one moment to the next who I was, I had lost me and I had no one to talk to. No one to ask if it really was me, if I really was that bad. Sometimes late at night I would let myself think for only brief moments that maybe I wasn't that bad and that he should just love me for who I am after all I hadn't changed into this person after I'd married him, or maybe I had.

My head would hurt for hours, I couldn't make sense of any of this on my own and yet I had no one to turn to. I couldn't phone my mother, we hadn't really been close for years any way Sam would monitor the phone calls., I'd never been given the chance to say how bad I felt. How sometimes I wanted to die, just so I could rest, just a little peace and quite oh what bliss that would be.

"What are you doing now?" Sam asked

"I'm just going in for a shower is that ok?" I asked, at least I had myself to talk to but wasn't that a sign of madness? Maybe Sam was right.

"Well go on then, you just mind you don't use a razor I need it to shave" he warned

As normal as I could hope to be, I grabbed a towel from the bedroom and headed for the kitchen still talking to myself, feeling slightly insane on the inside.

Standing in the shower I allowed myself to cry, this was the only time I was safe to do so, but I had to time it right. I had to make sure that I didn't spend to much time in the shower, after all how much time does it take to wash my crap brown hair?

That's when I noticed the scissors, I picked them up caressing the silver blades with my disgusting stubbly fingers. The pain inside me was unbearable, but I didn't want to die, or maybe I was just to weak to do it, but I had to do something. Carefully I held my left arm across my chest and drew the scissors up in my other hand. Bracing myself for the pain I began to score my left forearm back and forth stopping suddenly I realised that I was smiling the pain inside my head had gone, I felt better. Looking at my handy work, there was little blood just lots of neat little scratches all in a row, it didn't even hurt.

That's when I found my escape, I could do that when things were really bad, when I felt like I was about to explode. The pain inside me became bearable and it meant that I would on the outside at least I appeared normal, smiling and laughing. I had found some way of helping myself cope, I knew that it was wrong but at least while I was doing that I stopped wanting to die, because now I knew a way of helping to stop the pain. It wasn't a cry for help, I always had to wear clothes that showed no flesh so no one other than Sam would see them not that he would have cared anyway. If he were to ever ask I could just confirm what he thought of me, by telling me I'd tripped or been clumsy when hanging out the washing, I was always careful to do it I on different places on my body, but I favoured my left forearm it seemed to work better there.

18

I must have looked a sight that day, I remember it both scared and amused me, I'm not sure if it was then that realised I had lost my mind. It was a boiling hot day and Sam had allowed me to wear a dress with spaghetti straps. After all I had done all the house work and been shopping so there was no chance of me leaving the house again that day. There was no chance of any one seeing my revolting shape in the dress therefore there was no chance of embarrassing Sam, that of course was the most important thing. I shouldn't be bitter, he was in a fairly good mood and he let me wear a dress, I like to think that maybe he realised how much pain my bruises were giving me, he wasn't to know what was going to happen.

Sam, me and Paul were sat around the breakfast bar having a drink, Sam seemed happy, I can't remember why, it meant that for the time being at least he would leave me alone.

There was a knock at the door,

"Hello mate" came the voice followed by a man that I don't remember meeting.

"Alright" Sam responded, turning to face him, "this is the wife and this is my cousin"

"Bloody hell what you been doing to her ? Beating her up?" he said nodding in my direction.

Surprised I looked down at my self, Sam and Paul both looked at me. Maybe we had all just become used to seeing the bruises, that

108

they hadn't thought of making me go into another room when he had entered the kitchen. But now it was too late there I was in all my techno coloured glory. I had one enormous angry purple bruise that covered my right forearm from my shoulder to my elbow. Numerous smaller bruises of different sizes and ages covered my chest and legs..

"Yeah right mate, she's just fucking clumsy" Sam said laughing.

"Yeah clumsy" I agreed.

Smiling at them I watched as they disappeared into the sunroom, suddenly it all started to make sense. All I had wanted for so long was to ask someone if I was going insane. The answer was staring me in the face and it took a stranger to point it out to me. It must look so obvious to other people, I wasn't going insane. Sam wanted me to cover up my body not because it was ugly but because he didn't want anyone to see what he had done. It all made sense, silly I know but up and until that point I wasn't sure what to believe. I knew that I wasn't perfect but that didn't make me a bad person. I knew there and then I had to get away, and there wasn't anything that was going to change my mind, I slept well that night, even after another teaching session lesson from Sam for embarrassing him.

19

Sept 2002

"What's done is done, It's all water under the bridge, Time heals all wounds" all sayings that I'm sure someone would say to me if I had the courage to talk to someone. Looking around me, the other passengers were restless waiting to land. Thirty-six hours seems like a life time to some, for me it was eternity. I had spent a long time planning my escape, from the moment the stranger had enlightened me I knew what I had to do. Even so it had still taken me two months, three weeks and four days to do what I had done and now I needed it to be over. I needed to return to the safety of my family, to be able to take each day as it came.

The announcement came, we would be landing in twenty minutes. Twenty minutes and I would be on the relative safety of British soil. Sam and the life that I had would thousands of miles away. What lays ahead I don't know, one thing I needed was for those that I cared about to know what I had been through, to understand what I had been through to understand I had tried to be the best wife.

As the plane taxied along the runway the urge to move began to take over my body. I had before been a patient flyer, waiting to be told when I could move. Now though I needed to move, I want off this plane, off it now. Unbuckling my belt I stood, along with the other impatient souls. Time was moving too slowly,

"Please stop" the words left my mouth in a whisper.

The plane finally came to a rest. Grabbing my gear I forced my way onto the aisle. It was no good just being there I needed to move. In the tide of humans, I followed, not allowing anyone to cut in front of me. Its my time now, my time.

"Mrs Williams"

Turning I saw the kindly stewardess

"I'm going home" I told her in a whisper

"But were supposed to take you" she countered

"I'm going home" again as I spoke those words my heart lifted.

"Thank you" I called after her as I forced my way through, I'm going home, home. A place where I can be me. I can talk without fear. I can eat without shame. I can be free.

Moving from one foot to another I was acutely aware that no one stood near me, why/, because I stank. I don't care, why should I? All I had to do now was wait for my bag then walk through the doors to where I was told my mother would be waiting. My mother, it had been so long, I've missed so much of my families life's. There it was, hidden by other bags, but there it was. Grabbing it I manhandled it onto my trolley. I had already noted where the exit was and now I was heading towards it as fast as I could. The door was the entrance to my new life.

Fear was taking over again, there were my fellow passengers being greeted by their loved ones but still I walked on my own.

"Angharad"

Turning I saw her, she was different, she looked beautiful, letting go of the trolley I went to her, mums always make things better. Holding me tightly to her I wanted to cry but no tears came it didn't matter though I had my mum. Gently but forcefully she pulled me up,

"Hello"

Turning I saw my mum's partner, happy that he still looked like a big cuddly teddy bear I smiled. He'd taken hold of my bag, I'd always known my mum had made the right choice with him.

"Shall we go?" my mum asked

"Yes, yes, god I need a fag" I said laughing.

Walking through the car park, I pulled out my crumbled packet and rightly or wrongly enjoyed my first fag in thirty-six hours. I had landed at Heathrow, but still my journey wasn't over. I still had a four hour drive ahead of me but that didn't matter. We stopped not that long after for food, I'd explained that I hadn't eaten much on the plane and was starving. I sat with a fry up in front of me but only managed a few mouthfuls. I couldn't take my eyes off my mum, I half expected it all to be a dream. The conversations that we had, I can't remember I was tired and needed to sleep.

Laying alone the back seat, I heard them talking, my mum was saying that she was worried that maybe I would go back to him.

"What you don't know mum, is this isn't the first time I've left him but it will be the last" I spoke with such conviction that I frightened even myself.

"But how do you feel?" she asked

"Relieved mum, relieved that its all over" I replied before drifting off to sleep.

My mum, partner, sister and one of my brothers now lived in Yorkshire. My mum as a Yorkshire Lass had gone home and now as a Yorkshire Born I was going home. Even if it was a place that I had never been. Looking around this new place, it enchanted me, somewhere no one knows my name.

"Not long now"

"Who will be there?" I asked excitedly

"You're brother and sister are waiting"

My heart beating faster.

Pulling up outside, an amazing three storey house, I climbed out from the back seat.

The cold autumn air attacking my body, I had forgotten how bitterly cold English weather could be.

Walking into the lounge I was greeted by my brother, his baby girl and partner, my sister and her friend. My sister had grown into a beautiful young women and I had missed a huge chunk of that journey. My brother was now a father, their lives had moved on and I'd missed that. I had so much to tell them and so many questions to ask them. Now though I had the time.

20

Sat all wrapped up I watched the waves crash into the pier. I've been in England two weeks, but the peace I thought that I would feel hadn't arrived. Most nights I woke screaming or crying or both. Sam phoned everyday, switching from begging me to go home to threatening me if I didn't. I know he's capable of killing me, his family are well know as are his friends. I know the things that the Family will allow me to discuss and the things that will cause my head to become detached from my body, he therefore still has the control.

Thinking back to my visit to the Doctors today, I laughed at what the doctor had said to me. I was underweight. Me, underweight, I've spent so much energy believing myself to be fat, but no I was underweight. Sam had lied to me and I had let him. The only place I felt peace was at the beach, normally I went there when it was dark in order to have the place to myself. Now though the pier was busy, a Saturday in a British seaside resort. Too many people, it made me feel uncomfortable but I knew that I had to readjust to life.

Before I'd left the house my sister had asked me what I wanted for my Birthday and I couldn't answer her. Now though I knew. In a few weeks I will be 21 years old, 21. I feel 40 plus but my body will be 21. When I stand tall I'm 5 foot 6, with long brown hair right down my back. One day I hope to be able to look in the mirror and love what I see, scars included. I hope to smile at least once every day. I hope to be proud of myself. For now I hope to be able to wake each morning, to keep breathing all day long and to sleep the night through. With the knowledge that I have of my husbands dealings I am now a problem to him. He had told me that while I remain his wife I can't be made to testify against him. The game has now changed the rules are different. Trust no one because the Family has arms that can reach me any where. Getting up from the bench I made my way through the crowds. How is it possible to be so alone when surrounded by so many? For now I just need to put one foot in front of the other. Build up my strength for the next time I see him, because whenever that day is, it will surly arrive. No different to the sun rising every morning.

About the Author

Angharad married the man she loved only for her heart and mind to be left broken after he stole from her, her love of life. Angharad knew that she had to be the perfect wife but unable to achive what he wanted, she was punished.

Angharad now lives in deepest darkest Yorkshire sharing her days with her family, her new and loving partner, his family and her beloved cat, Schannps. Most none working hours are spent avoiding housework especially ironing, only submitting to these tasks when carefully placed suggestions written in inch thick dust or the disapproving looks of her beloved Schannps entice her towards the cleaning products hiding under the sink.

Printed in the United Kingdom
by Lightning Source UK Ltd.
117795UK00001B/196